CALL ME AMERICAN

CALL ME AMERICAN

THE EXTRAORDINARY TRUE STORY OF A YOUNG SOMALI IMMIGRANT

ABDI NOR IFTIN

WITH MAX ALEXANDER

EMBER

In Chapters 15 and 16, some names of individuals have been changed to protect their privacy.

Visit us on the Web! GetUnderlined.com

Educators and librarians, for a variety of teaching tools, visit us at RHTeachersLibrarians.com

The Library of Congress has cataloged the hardcover edition of this work as follows:
Names: Iftin, Abdi Nor, author. | Alexander, Max.
Title: Call me American / Abdi Nor Iftin, with Max Alexander.
Other titles: Call me American (Delacorte Press)
Description: First edition. | New York, NY : Delacorte Press, 2020. | Audience: Grades 9–12. |
Audience: Ages 12+
Identifiers: LCCN 2019018309 (print) | LCCN 2019019083 (ebook) |
ISBN 978-1-9848-9712-1 (el) | ISBN 978-1-9848-9711-4 (hc)
Subjects: LCSH: Iftin, Abdi Nor—Juvenile literature. | Somali Americans—Biography—
Juvenile literature. | Somali Americans—Maine—Biography—Juvenile literature. |
Immigrants—Maine—Biography—Juvenile literature. | Muslims—Maine—Biography—
Juvenile literature. | Children and war—Somalia—Juvenile literature. | Somalia—
History—1991—Juvenile literature. | Mogadishu (Somalia)—Biography—Juvenile literature.
Classification: LCC CT275.I43 (ebook) | LCC CT275.I43 A3 2020 (print) |
DDC 305.893/540741—dc23

ISBN 978-1-9848-9713-8 (pbk.)

Printed in the United States of America
3rd Printing
First Ember Edition 2021

This book is for my proud nomad mother, who saved me. Mom, you nursed my bloody feet after I had walked for miles with you without shoes; you gave me hope with your stories of brave life in the bush; and when I rested my head on a graveyard full of kids of my age, you would not let me join them. Your strength kept me alive in the city of the dead. Now I am safe in America. So long as we both live, I will return that strength and support to you.

A mule that grazes with horses thinks it is a horse.

—Somali proverb

CONTENTS

INTRODUCTION

Since I arrived in America in 2014, I have had the privilege of meeting and speaking with students all over this country; they always have so many good questions—some of them hard to answer!—which can only come from strong curiosity about the world.

My world as a kid was very different from yours, but I had the same passion to see beyond my horizon. On the streets of Mogadishu, Somalia—hungry, scared, without shoes or much hope for a future—my own curiosity about the world kept me going. In Hollywood movies, which I watched on a small TV screen in a dirt-floored shack, I saw American kids and teenagers, and I dreamed of their life. I wanted toys, freshly made beds, a refrigerator full of food, a roof over my head, clean clothes, schools and teachers. I couldn't have those things, but I pretended I was an American boy and even called myself Abdi American.

This did not make my parents happy. They had grown

up as simple but proud nomadic herdspeople, roaming across hundreds of miles of bush land with their animals. They played on the hot sand, drank fresh camel milk, and chanted songs around fires at night to ward off the lions and hyenas. My mother and father both have scars from fights with those wild animals. Despite the dangers, they were totally free people. They had no laws other than what they believed God commanded; they owned only what they could carry; they had no traffic lights, no insurance policies, not even money.

But when a drought took their herd, they were forced to move to the big city where I was born. I did not grow up tending camels and cows, but every night my parents told me stories of that world so I would not forget where I came from.

I am proud of my nomad heritage, but I did not choose to be born in Somalia. No one gets a choice. It could have been you who was born in Somalia and lost everything at the age of five. It could have been you who wandered in the wilderness for months with sore and bloody feet, an empty belly, surrounded by hungry animals and brutal soldiers. Of course no child deserves what I went through. But it could happen to anyone.

You could say my story has a happy ending because I got out of that terrible place and now live in America. But my story includes my family, still in Africa, struggling to survive every day. They are lucky that I can support them, but I can't go there, nor can I protect them from the daily risk of sickness and violence.

Luck is a funny thing. I have had bad luck and good luck in my life. Either way, I always tried to be prepared when good luck came my way. So I taught myself English while watching those Hollywood movies, even though there was no use for English in Mogadishu—in fact, speaking English there could be dangerous if the wrong people heard you. Then one day, English came in handy and changed my life. If you take one lesson from this book, I hope it's that every life has some good luck and bad luck; what matters is what you make of it.

When I speak to school groups across America, I don't like telling young people they should be thankful for being born in a free and peaceful country, because it sounds like we should take pity on the less fortunate, or be sorry for their existence. The poor and desperate people of the world don't want our pity. Unlike me, most don't even want to become American. Like my parents, they cherish their own heritage and culture. They only want a fair chance, as fellow human beings on this planet. They don't want the random accident of their birthplace to mean a death sentence.

I know there are no easy solutions to the problems of the world. But a good place to start is understanding—and that comes from listening to each other's stories. As you read my story, I encourage you to think about your own story, and what you would say about yourself to people in faraway places like Somalia. Listen to your parents' and grandparents' stories; whether your ancestors were Native Americans or immigrants from Italy or enslaved people from West Africa or Pilgrims from England, they all have something to teach us. You can live in a small remote town or a big noisy city, in America or Europe or Africa or beyond. Wherever you live, wherever you come from, your story matters. We are all connected by our stories.

1

UNDER THE NEEM TREE

I was born under a neem tree, probably in 1985. Neem trees grow everywhere in Somalia, with fragrant blossoms like lilacs and medicinal bitter sap that heals sores. People everywhere in Somalia brush their teeth with those twigs. Their green fruit turns yellow and juicy, a tasty treat for the birds. The trees' limbs spread wide and give shelter from the sun—a good place to have a baby. A good place to be born.

I was born into a culture where birthdays are not celebrated, or even recorded. This became a problem for me when I left Somalia and entered the world of documents and paperwork. My first birthday record was in Kenya at a refugee registration center. The officers there did not bother to ask me when I was born, because they know Somalis have no idea. They simply wrote down my birthday as January 1, 1985. To them, every Somali is born on New Year's Day.

Arriving in America was different. Here the officials said I had to come up with a birth date and stick with it for the rest of my life. It's a strange thing to choose your own birthday. But there I was. I chose a date around the middle of the year, which would be equally close to whatever my real birthday was: June 20, 1985.

My parents don't know the day of my birth, but my mom remembers it was very hot. The blazing sun had turned the streets of Mogadishu ash white and the rooms of our small block house into bread ovens. Mom was under the shade of the neem tree, resting on a *jiimbaar*, a bed made of cow leather stretched over sticks. Our neighbor Maryan cooled Mom's head with a fan woven from straw, and cleaned the blood. The women of the neighborhood brought fragrant resins and incense like myrrh and *uunsi*. For me they brought *xildiid*, the root of a plant that is mixed with water to bathe and protect the baby.

Somalia was once called the Land of the Perfumes; before the wars began, my country exported fragrant and medicinal plants all over the world. My mom remembers *somagale*, a seasonal plant that sprouts from the ground in the rainy season. She would uproot the plants, crush them, and apply the paste to any wounds. Mom still believes in those traditional plants that cure everything. She believes knowledge of them has helped her survive anywhere. My mom worried I would not be as strong as her because people in the city don't know how to survive off the land. I tell her I have learned other ways to survive.

The moment I appeared, Maryan ran down the street to

break the good news to my dad that a boy was born (boys are much more appreciated than girls in Somalia). My dad took a day off from work and partied with his friends, buying them qat leaves, a stimulant like strong coffee chewed by men in Arabia and the Horn of Africa. Somali culture dictated that my dad had to stay away from the house while my mother was giving birth; he would stay at his friend Siciid's place for forty days, the amount of time a woman is supposed to remain chaste after labor. He visited us, as a guest in his own house, during the day. Mom was still sleeping under the neem tree, near clay bowls and glass jars full of porridge and orange juice. Out of respect for my dad she covered her hair while he was there, looking down as she answered his questions. They would never kiss or hug in public. He stood tall and aloof from her bed, examining me, his second son, lying next to Mom.

The women perfumed the rooms of the house and swept the yard bent over, using a short broom. They came in and out. That same evening, Maryan walked in with ten men, all of them respected local religious leaders in the community, known as sheikhs. They wore beaded necklaces and beards. They circled the *jiimbaar* in the yard where I was lying next to Mom. Some women were cooking a big pot of camel meat; others were mixing a jar of camel milk with sugar and ice cubes from the store. Camel meat and sweet milk together are called *duco*, a blessing for the newborn. For an hour the sheikhs blessed me, verse after verse, very loud, which makes the blessing greater. Afterward, they all sat on a mat on the ground, washed their hands in a dish of water, and feasted on the camel meat and milk. This blessing and feast meant I would grow better, be healthy and obedient to my parents.

Soon after I was born, Mom went back to doing her housework, with me tied to her back so that she was there for me whenever I cried out for milk. She watched me crawl out of the shade of that same neem tree into the scorching heat of the sun, and she was there when I took my first steps on the hot dusty ground. At bedtime she told me Somali folktales and sang lullabies like "Huwaaya Huwaa." Mom and her stories were my universe.

Mom likes to call herself the brave daughter of her brave parents. Her name is Madinah Ibrahim Moalim. She was named Madinah after the holy city in Saudi Arabia, where the Prophet Muhammad is buried. It was her parents' biggest dream to visit Mecca and Madinah, to make the pilgrimage known as the *hajj*, but unfortunately, they never got to. Mom too wants to visit before she dies. Growing up with a huge number of Somali exiles returning from Saudi Arabia, I never understood why my family wished to see a place where Somalis are unwelcome. It would be many years before I realized that Somalis are pretty much unwelcome everywhere, and dreams are all we have.

■ ■ ■

When Mom was growing up, her parents were always moving with the goats and camels. It must have been a little before Somalia got independence from the Italians in 1960. She never saw Italian or British colonialists—the Europeans who had taken over the land—but remembers her parents talking about people with no skin that they had seen driving back and forth. Mom says it does not matter how old she is, but she knows she is as old as her camel Daraanle, who was also born the day she was. Her family had almost five hundred camels, goats, and cows in total. They didn't know how to count with numbers, but they named and marked every one and could keep track of them by their names. They provided the family with milk, meat, and transportation, but there were far more animals than they needed for food. Somali herdspeople have no permanent home, no belongings besides clothes, some jewelry, and cooking utensils. Their wealth is the size of their herd. They have no insurance payments, no loans, no future plans, nothing to worry about except lions and hyenas. To them, there are only two days: the day you are born, and the day you die. Everything in between is herding animals.

My grandparents on both sides were proud pastoralists, people of the land. They herded their animals across the Bay region in south central Somalia, always moving to find water. They had never heard of Mogadishu, the capital of Somalia, or even Somalia itself, much less Nairobi or New York. The Bay region lies between the Jubba and the Shabelle Rivers, which nourish the soil. It has more livestock than anywhere else in Somalia and is famous for its gorgeous Isha Baidoa waterfall. The wide grazing land was all they knew.

Nomads of Bay region enjoy two rainy seasons over the year: *Dayr*, with light rains, begins in mid-October; *gu* brings heavy rains in mid-April. As the clouds build, the animals can smell the coming rain and they dance in anticipation. The people see the excitement of the animals, and they raise their hands to thank God: *"Alhamdulilah!"*

The rains mean plentiful water, so the nomads can finally settle down for a few months and build their makeshift huts from sticks carried on the backs of camels. At night the animals stay close to the hut in their corral, and the families sit around a fire near them. They dance with songs for the animals. There is laughter and fresh water and joy. A good time for stories, folktales, poems, and delicious meals of corn and meat. In his time, Iftin, my grandfather, would tell his own brave stories. He would talk about the day he met a pride of lions face to face near his house and chased them away for a mile. Eventually, the rains stop, the water dries up, and the nomads pack up and move on.

My parents as well as grandparents could name their own great-great-great-grandparents; they could spend a whole night telling the stories they have passed down. All these ancestral names carry pride; every single one of them was a brave man or woman, someone who owned many livestock and was well known in the area and probably killed a lion. My parents never talked about their lives without talking about the lives of their parents and ancestors because, to Somali nomads, there is no individual life, only the life of your family. And like their ancestors, my parents followed the Muslim rules. Women have to respect their husbands. Men have power over everything. My parents never questioned these rules or how they came about.

My mom, Madinah, was a very beautiful nomad girl, tall and slim, with dark hair, a long neck, and beautiful eyes. One summer day at a watering hole somewhere in Bay region, my dad, Nur Iftin, and his herd encountered my mom and hers.

My dad says he could not take his eyes off my mom. He had never seen such a beautiful woman. Mom was barefoot, wearing her long *guntiino* dress, which goes over only one shoulder, a necklace of black wooden beads, and metal bands around her upper arms. The scars on her neck and arms said without words how brave she was fighting wild animals.

They were both proud members of the Rahanweyn clan. So when they met, it was friendly. Dad was in his *macawis*, a knee-length cloth wrapped tightly around his waist. He wore his nomad sandals made of animal leather. His camels mixed with Mom's goats around the watering hole. He approached her, and he bragged about his wealth, the animals, which is the only pickup line in the nomadic culture.

My mom liked him at first sight. Not many men were even taller than my tall mom, but he towered over her. He had a scar on his forehead that showed he had also wrestled wild animals. His high Afro hairstyle crowned his head and wide shoulders. His dusty feet showed that he had walked miles and was still not tired. As he stood there, he introduced Mom to his favorite camels, naming them as they grazed. They also had names for the wild animals that threatened their herds. They talked about Fareey, a local lion who had been terrorizing the herds. Fareey was named for his missing toe, which made his footprints in the clay distinct. Fareey and his pride killed many animals, including some belonging to my parents' families, after dark. My dad swore that he would find Fareey and his pride and kill them all to protect my mom's goats. He never did find that lion, but it was a way to show my mom that he could care for her.

After their first brief meeting, my parents searched for each other for a couple of months. When they finally met at another watering hole, my dad believed his prayers had been answered. Now Nur Iftin could not hide his love for Madinah and said he wanted to marry her. She did not say yes or no, but grinned and looked down coyly. It was a yes.

Dad arranged a meeting with her parents, and one day both families met in a place near Baidoa, the biggest city in the region, where the agreement was negotiated: fifty camels as a dowry, the price my dad's parents paid to my mom's parents.

The wedding happened in a town called Hudur, about sixty miles from Baidoa. This was the rainy season, so the animals were fat, and there was so much meat and milk at the wedding. Mom was in a mud hut all day with what they called the expert women, who told her stories about what would happen on the wedding night. It was a rented hut; they had to deposit goats to stay there. Neither of them had ever seen a banknote or a coin. At the same time, my dad was in a neighbor's hut with the men teaching him about the first days of marriage.

My parents spent most of their early marriage walking

miles every day into no-man's territory with their herds. No one stopped them or asked who they were. It was a peaceful time. The land beneath their feet was scorching hot. They believed Earth was flat and that it was Allah's land; they were only guests. It rains when Allah wills, it turns dry when Allah wills. Animals and humans die when Allah wills.

In the bush, nomadic Somali men and women work together, talk freely with each other, and even play games together. To survive on the land, a husband and wife must work as a team to make sure their animals are grazed well and that they all get back home by dusk. My dad had introduced my mom to several games, like high jump, sprint running, and chasing dik-diks, the little antelopes not much bigger than a cat. They would hold sticks five feet high, then take turns jumping over them. Mom learned to jump and land without stumbling. Mom was shy and respectful to her husband, but when it came to games and fun, she was a fierce competitor. They sprinted together across the bush, leaping over thornbushes while chasing the fast dik-diks.

Bay region is famous in Somalia for growing corn, beans, rice, sesame, papayas, mangoes, and the tree that produces frankincense resin. Most of that resin is bought by the Catholic church in Rome, but my parents knew nothing of Rome or Christianity. To them the most amazing place in the world was the Isha Baidoa waterfall. It was like their vacationland. During their nomadic travels they stopped twice a year to shower under the gushing water.

The city of Baidoa is called Baidoa the Paradise for both the nearby waterfall and the fertile red soil. Corn and *masago*, a type of grain, grow among the mango and banana trees. In the center of town is the huge Afar Irdoodka market, where people come from all across the country to buy and sell food, medicinal herbs, and supplies. Everywhere in that city, donkeys loaded with supplies are moving toward the market.

The Rahanweyn tribe live in Baidoa and on all the land between and surrounding the Jubba and Shabelle Rivers. The word *Rahanweyn* translates into "large number." There are so many of them, spread across the bush. To most of the other Somali tribes, the Rahanweyn are looked down on because they are mostly nomads and poor and have nothing to do with politics. Also, the dialect the Rahanweyn speak, called Maay, is dismissed as the speech of beggars and the lower class. It is different in sentence structure and is complex to outsiders. So, for centuries, the Rahanweyn lived their own life, on land belonging to no one.

Soon after my parents' wedding, in 1977, a terrible drought hit Somalia. The corn withered. The red clay land around Baidoa turned parched and bare, and became littered with animals' skeletons. Those that survived were thin and dying. The nomads knew it was God's choice but could not understand why he would do this, because they were not sinful people. They decided Allah wanted the animals for himself and was taking them away. My parents, who had been so proud of their herds, watched their wealth wiped out in front of their eyes. Daraanle, my mom's favorite camel, died.

Droughts were a part of life for nomads in Bay region, but

new forces in the world made this drought different. That same year, Somalia attacked Ethiopia in a war over control of the Ogaden territory, a part of Ethiopia that is populated mainly by ethnic Somalis. Somalia deployed troops to the border, with tanks and military vehicles. My parents had never seen anything like them, they had never even thought about such a thing as a government or an army. They didn't know it, but under the dictator Mohammed Siad Barre, the founder of Somalia's Supreme Revolutionary Council, their country had amassed the largest army in Africa. Siad Barre was a general who had taken over in 1969. He had also cleverly used the Cold War to gain support from the Soviet Union.

The 1977 war, known as the Ogaden War, was the bloodiest ever between two African nations. There were tens of thousands of casualties. That huge Somali army unleashed its heavy weaponry and Soviet-trained soldiers against the Ethiopians in a massive attack over the border. In the beginning, the Somalis advanced deep into Ethiopia, almost capturing the capital, Addis Ababa. But things got more complicated. The Soviet Union *also* supported Ethiopia, which had a Marxist military regime, and tried to stop the war. When Siad Barre refused to back down, the Soviets abandoned Somalia and sided with Ethiopia, a much larger country. Then the war became global. China, Yemen, North Korea, Romania, and other nations got involved, supporting either side. With the Soviet Union supplying the Ethiopian Air Force with weaponry, the Somali army was pushed out of the country and defeated in 1978. Siad Barre was furious. Wanting a buffer against a Soviet-backed Ethiopia, the Americans—who were strictly anti-Soviet—rushed into the vacuum and began to give military help to Somalia. But if it had not been for the American support, Siad Barre might have been driven out of power for his needless and costly war. Instead, he was able to build up his army again.

All these shifting alliances and power plays meant nothing to my parents. But the result—a small country with millions of guns and simmering resentment against Siad Barre for causing so much misery—would soon change their lives forever.

Meanwhile, the 1977 drought wiped out lives and displaced tens of thousands of nomads. As the animals died, some nomads started moving, mostly toward Kenya and Ethiopia. Others moved to the nearest cities with fishing and other work opportunities. And so my parents decided to try for a better life in the Somali capital of Mogadishu. After fifteen days of walking and begging rides, they set foot for the first time in a city with movie theaters, traffic lights, houses made of bricks, and citizens who spoke a completely different dialect. The green and red taxicabs that parked everywhere, the portraits of Siad Barre that hung on every street, it all caught them by surprise. They would later learn that you weren't supposed to say Siad Barre's name without adding the word *jaalle* before it. *Jaalle* was a new word in the Somali language invented by Siad Barre, which roughly meant "führer" or "leader."

My dad's half brother Hassan, who already lived in Mogadishu, gave my parents a room in his house. A mile from their house, to the east, was the Mogadishu airport and the beautiful green waters of the Indian Ocean surrounding it. But mom missed the animals, her parents, the stories, the land, her freedom. She had not slept in weeks due to the sound of the airplanes taking off and landing. Her first visit to the ocean made her remember stories from her parents, including one about something called a whale that can swallow a whole city. She worried about whales, and she wondered where the ocean ends. Using a toilet, going to a movie, and riding a bus were the strangest things to both my parents, probably the way so many things about America would one day seem strange to me, like snow, cooking on a stove, or obeying traffic laws.

One thing that frustrated her more than anything else was buying milk and meat. In her nomad life, these things were abundant; now she had to pay for them with money. My mom was an expert on camel meat, and she could tell this meat sold in stores was not fresh, but she didn't dare to question the scary butchers with their long knives and strange dialect.

The city people made fun of the nomads. My mom remembers other women asking her to make sounds of animals. They were mocking her, but animals were her favorite subject, so she was happy to make their sounds. The city women, who wore nicer clothes, did not want to be seen with Mom. To them, she was a little embarrassing. They mocked her dialect, looking down on her whenever she said something in Maay. She was called *Reer Baadiye*, "the bush woman."

The neighbors said her house smelled like goat pee, from her clothes. To Mom, the smell of goats and camels was like the perfume of her homeland, and it smelled like freedom. Also she had learned only a handful of verses from the Koran that her parents had taught her, just enough to pray five times a day. The city women, who had studied at madrassas (schools teaching the Koran), knew the whole text by heart. But none of those women could jump or run like my mom. They were too plump from all the city food, and they avoided sunshine so they would get lighter skin.

Soon enough, my dad started making money fishing, and he and mom left Hassan's house to rent their own room. Fishermen would go out in boats with big nets while my dad stayed on Uruba beach, waiting for them to return with their big nets full. Dad would carry the huge, heavy fish a mile to the fish market at Geel-Laq beach, some days making that trip dozens of times. After a whole day of that hard work, he was supposed to get paid one Somali shilling, but he still didn't know much about money or coins and was often cheated.

At that time, there were still Italians in Mogadishu. Before independence came in 1960, Somalia was two colonies: British Somaliland in the north and Italian Somaliland, including Mogadishu, in the south. So there was a long history of Europeans in Somalia, and in the 1970s and 1980s many still came to do business. They stayed in the big Uruba Hotel, today in ruins. It was the first time Dad saw white people, and he couldn't believe they walked around in bikinis, almost naked. When he told my mom, she couldn't believe it either; she had to come and see for herself. Even then, she didn't believe they were real people until she saw them actually breathing. Mom in her nomad life had heard stories about *gaalo*, the infidels. They are not Muslim, they are all white, and they are not clean. She avoided them and wondered, *What are they doing here, and why don't they pray five times a day?*

Everywhere in Mogadishu, my dad stood out in the crowd with his strong body and height. He had cut his long nomad hair short and shaved his nomad's beard, but he left his dark mustache and woolly sideburns. This look was very fashionable in Mogadishu in the early 1980s, especially if you also wore bell-bottoms. He would go out and strut around town. There were more nightclubs than mosques in Mogadishu back then, all places where you could dance to funk music. Some Somali men and even some women went to clubs to mingle with the Europeans before the civil war. Eventually, my dad did go to the Uruba Club, though he never told my mom. Today those clubs, like the hotel, are rubble in the sand.

The fishing and dancing might have gone on for my dad until the wars came, but then one day he did something that changed his life. He jumped.

It was nothing to him, just jumping over a thorn fence, like in those games with my mom in the bush. But this jump was seen by a friend of his half brother Hassan, who knew a lot about basketball. That game had become very popular all over Africa. Hassan's friend said that because my dad was so tall and could jump so high, he should try out for the national basketball team. Dad knew nothing about basketball, had never even held a ball. But Hassan's friend wouldn't give up. The Somali national team was recruiting new players.

So my dad tried out for basketball and was a natural. He towered over his teammates. He could jump higher and had strong hands from working with animals. His herding skills also made him very agile and gave him stamina. It didn't take long for him to get used to handling the ball. Soon he was nicknamed Nur Dhere, "Tall Nur," and he was helping Somalia win games. He stopped carrying fish and started making a lot more money. The world changed swiftly for my parents. They learned how to count shilling notes and coins and how to buy things like clothes, curtains, window shutters made of wood, a carpet over their dirt floor, a cupboard, and a shelf. Things only rich people had. My dad also learned to read and write Somali, which was unusual because nomad men and women were mostly illiterate.

By the time I was born, my parents had become famous all over Mogadishu. Dad was traveling a lot outside the country, bringing medals home. He had a shortwave radio in the house and would listen to songs by famous Somali singers. My nomad parents had a lot of good things happening, but my mom missed everything in the nomad world. She thought that city life was hard and resented having to stay inside a house all day, cooking and cleaning, instead of herding her goats across the landscape, while Dad was out playing basketball. She was worried that my older brother, my younger sister, and I would grow up in Mogadishu not knowing anything about the life of nomads.

Dad spent most of his time away from home, training with the basketball squad. Usually he returned on Thursday for two days (Friday being the holy day), still wearing his red Somali team shirt and bringing gifts of clothes and toys for us, sometimes jewelry for Mom. He would sit with our neighbor Siciid under the neem tree in the evening, talking late into the night. Siciid looked short compared to Dad, a smile constantly fixed to his round face. Like Mom, he told many stories and also jokes, and he provoked Dad into arguments, just for the fun of it. Siciid was a professional driver who earned his living delivering food and oil for the government. Mom would bring them tea outside while they chatted.

Sometimes, Dad took me to watch him train at the Horseed Stadium in downtown Mogadishu. Mom dressed me up with a nice clean vest and shorts. The court was behind a thick concrete wall, and fans would climb up a tall tree to get a view. They sat there for hours watching as my dad and his teammates, the best in Somalia, played basketball all afternoon. I had the honor to walk into the building with my dad holding my tiny hand in his big one. People greeted him like a star. Police and soldiers saluted him like he was a general. Dad played for hours, and eventually I would fall asleep on the stairs, only waking on his shoulders as he carried me home.

We'd walk home in the evening past the big traffic island

at KM4 Street, the Cinema Ecuatore, and shops and restaurants bursting with laughter, music, and discussion. People talked about concerts and plays. The famous Waberi entertainment club presented great shows and comedians on Friday that would crack people up. I had no idea then that they'd all be gone so soon.

In the old part of town, above the ruins of the medieval sultanates' castles, rose the white spires of the ancient Arba'a Rukun mosque and the Catholic cathedral, which had been built by the Italians. We could see the ocean beyond the Almara lighthouse, built of stone in the fifteenth century when Mogadishu was a major African port, and we felt the power of the sea breeze against our faces. *Mogadishu is a great city*, I thought, *maybe the greatest in the world*. I felt so lucky.

•••

My earliest memories of Mogadishu always include my brother, Hassan, named after my uncle. He was a hero to me, only one year older but always my protector from the other boys in the neighborhood who tried to bully me. Hassan was without fear and would fight with boys older than himself; sometimes he would fight with three at the same time, returning home covered in cuts and dust. On one occasion, I was attacked by two boys who threw me to the ground, then punched and kicked me. I didn't tell my mom, but I did tell Hassan, who went after them and beat them. When we weren't roughing it up, we played fun games like hide-and-seek, *gariir* (a type of marbles game using rocks), and blindman's bluff.

Hassan went to the madrassa, where he learned the Koran with eighty other boys sitting on the sand in a shack. There was no paper; the students wrote on long wooden boards, using ink made from coal. They wrote a passage from the Koran in Arabic, memorized and repeated it, then washed off the ink and wrote the next passage. All day they did this. Mistakes were severely punished by the teacher, a scowling bearded man named Macalin Basbaas, roughly translated as "the teacher who uses hot pepper and scorpions to bite on wounds." Never was someone better named. Hassan returned home bleeding from the beatings he got.

The madrassas were the only kind of school in Mogadishu, and there was nothing to learn there except the Koran. So my mom became my greatest teacher. She could cook, bake, and sing, but what I loved most about her were the tales she told us about her nomadic youth, her time as a herdswoman in the desert scrub. She would sit cross-legged under the neem tree with Hassan and me while our baby sister, Nima, slept with her thumb in her mouth.

Mom told us about the day when a hyena suddenly appeared, growling and gnashing teeth. She chased it with her stick through the scrub before returning to her goats and camels, knowing she should get them to the corral near her parents before darkness, when more hyenas would come out. But the pack had already scattered the herd. Without fear she chased them, for Somalis value their goats and camels as much as their own lives. A hyena leaped at her, pinning her to the ground, its sharp claws cutting into her neck. Luckily, her uncle arrived and started striking the hyena with a stick. Mom was unstoppable, though. A few days later, still in great pain, she went right back to minding the herd.

My head rested on her lap, looking up at the hyena scar on her neck. She still wore the necklace she had on when she met my dad—black beads made from hard, polished wenge wood, the sort worn by women in the bush but rarely seen in the city. I wondered how my quiet mom, who hid in the house when men visited, could chase hyenas.

The scariest story she told was about the night when a lion entered the hut where a relative was sleeping with his children. The hungry lion dragged the man out into the bush screaming and crying while his children slept. Mom was one of the people who came out of the huts armed with spears, but when they reached him, he was almost dead.

The story haunted me and gave me nightmares. I sometimes asked myself, "What if I was born a nomad?" Surely, I would be killed by a lion. I hated death. I just wanted to live a good life like the one we had and hang on my dad's shoulders walking around town being cheered. Mom told us these stories not to scare us but to help us understand life in the bush, to appreciate it. Her goal was to keep us from becoming city boys who know little about nomad life. She wanted us to not mock other nomads who came to the city but to respect them and listen to their stories. We were also able to learn and speak the nomadic Rahanweyn dialect because Mom told all her stories in Maay. She trained us in the house and courtyard on how to fight, climb trees, and jump. Hassan and I could jump higher than most of the boys in the neighborhood.

It was around that same time when Dad told our family that the basketball games were finished and he would be staying at home now. I didn't know how basketball could be finished. Wasn't there always another game, on another day? Soon I began to notice people were tense and there were lots of changes in our routines. Dad's friend Siciid was now with us most of the time, returning to his own house only to sleep and spending long hours with Dad listening to the radio. His wife and children had left Mogadishu and gone to stay with relatives in the north of Somalia. Like Dad, he had stopped going to work.

Dad and Siciid talked about politics. Since the end of the bloody Ogaden War with Ethiopia in 1978, Somalia's economy was weak. People were angry at President Siad Barre, especially the people around Mogadishu who were mainly from the Hawiye clan. Siad Barre came from the rival Darod clan up north. There were five major clans in Somalia, but since independence, the Hawiye and the Darod had nominated themselves as the only people who could be president or prime minister. My clan, the nomadic Rahanweyn clan, was not allowed to rule. Soon, instead of presidents and prime ministers, the Hawiye and the Darod would give us brutal warlords.

Before the Ogaden War, when he was still popular, Siad Barre managed to keep the Hawiye people under control, and he watched them carefully. One of their leaders, an army general named Mohamed Farrah Aidid, had been jailed for a time. Now he was free again and ready to fight his Darod rival, thanks to weapons and money he was getting from Ethiopia, which also hated Siad Barre because of the war. Aidid had whipped up the Hawiye of the rural areas, and that's where the fighting was going on. But how long could this fight stay out in the bush?

Of course, I was too young to understand any of this. For the first time ever, I saw that my dad's face was not happy. In his eyes I saw fear. This was a new thing to see, and while I understood it as part of something larger beginning, all I could think of was that everything I knew was ending.

2

THE FIRST BULLETS

Finally one day the fighters arrived, looting the shops and firing the first bullets of the bloody civil war. At night I heard bullets hitting the neem tree and the birds flying off in all directions. The next morning, I woke up to see mattresses, beds, food, basketballs, and Dad's basketball trophies all packed outside. Dad carried the most important things in a sack with one hand and a mattress in the other hand. Left behind were the sacks of flour, rice, and corn. Mom, now pregnant with her fourth child, carried our clothes, our sister's formula, milk, and a few cooking utensils, plus Nima on her back, wrapped in a big scarf the African way. Hassan and I trailed behind our parents on a dusty, scorching day with bullets and smoke all over the city.

After we walked just a few yards, I cried to be carried. Mom ignored me, instead reciting verses from the Koran while looking on both sides of the streets before we crossed. As we walked, I saw huge padlocks on the gates of houses I knew in the neighborhood; people had already fled. The locks meant they were hoping to return; maybe this would all blow over in a few weeks. Everywhere, I saw moms holding the hands of other kids my age, standing on the side of the road in shock. I heard screams and crying children. The small restaurant where I used to go with Dad, named for its owner, Hashi, was being looted. The food went quickly. Hashi belonged to the tribe of President Siad Barre, who had been ousted by those rebels. Mom worried about his whereabouts.

There was a crowd gathered a short distance from the restaurant, where a body lay facedown—the first corpse I would see. It turned out to be Hashi's body. Rebels laughed and threw their arms in the air in triumph, smashing the windows of shops with their rifle butts before racing each other to collect the most valuable pickings. Most of them wore a *macawis*, as my father used to wear in the bush. That's how we knew the rebels were not city people; they had come into town from the outlands and were probably seeing shops and restaurants for the first time, just as my parents had several years before.

When there was nothing left to loot from the shops, I saw people being robbed at gunpoint. On every street, buildings were on fire. A rebel in a pickup truck passed guns to a group of teenagers. The drivers honked and waved as soldiers in pickup trucks shook their rifles in the air and danced. Some jumped out and ran after us, holding a gun in one hand. All of them were very dark-skinned and thin. They called themselves nicknames based on their features, like gangsters I would see in Hollywood movies: Daga Weyne (Long-Eared), Afdheere (Long Mouth), or Ileey (One-Eyed).

"They are giving guns out like sweets!" Dad said. "Who is in charge of these people?"

With the civil war spreading into the city, some people managed to escape by boats, airplanes, ships, and even cars crossing into neighboring countries. Most of these people who escaped worked for the government. Some of my dad's own teammates got help from people in their tribes to get to America, Canada, or the United Kingdom. But no one had even contacted my dad. The country was divided by clans and tribes, and people helped only people they were related to by those groups. My dad's Rahanweyn clan were the farmers and nomads who could not help him escape. So my parents had to use their nomad skills to try to save us. What nomads do is walk.

And so we embarked on a walk that I will never forget. For years we called it the walk of death.

Seven miles of walking and we arrived at the house of our relative Mumin, who was a general in the Somali army. Mumin was my dad's cousin; he was the only man in our extended family to be in the army's highest ranks. He was educated, having studied in Mogadishu before joining the army. His house was behind a wall with a gate. Mumin appeared at the gate, his hands nervously scratching at his mustache. The blue Somali flag flew over his house. "There's no one who can stop the fighting," he said. "No one is talking to anyone else, just fighting." He looked at the flag and shook his head. President Siad Barre had already fled. The rebels seemed unstoppable, and a general like Mumin would be a certain target. "I must leave with my family because it's everyone for himself," he said. "I hope that you will be safe here." He wiped his fingers on my face and Hassan's, but our tears ran harder.

"We'll be all right here," Dad told Mumin. "We'll stay the night and move on in the morning."

So we slept in the home of a cousin who was a general in the defeated army, while rebels shot their way across the city, looking for government officials to kill. It did not seem very safe. The rooms of the house were all packed with neighbors and other Rahanweyn seeking shelter, so we slept outside. We laid our mattresses in the courtyard while Dad stayed near the gate. I heard the Rahanweyn dialect. People were scared; men like my dad were pacing back and forth, thinking of what to do. People were worried for their lives.

It was an uncomfortable night of blasts and mosquito bites. The back side of Mumin's house bordered on the largest Somali hospital, Madinah Hospital. That night the militias were busy looting the hospital, grabbing anything valuable to sell. We could hear the rebels looting and shouting; they kicked down doors and broke glass, even tore off the roof. We rose early to find bullet holes in the gate of Mumin's house, and we slipped away quietly.

...

The road south ran along the sea. Out on the waves, white ships like whales moved slowly in the distance. Later I found out these ships were evacuating government officials. They managed to protect themselves, without looking out for the rest of us. On the land, cows, donkeys, stray dogs, and chickens moved aimlessly through the crowds of people. A thin man painted the letters *USC*—United Somali Congress, the main militia group of Aidid—in white on every wall.

Dad told us to go back and stay at Mumin's and that he would go try to find Siciid, who maybe still had his truck and could take us to Baidoa. While we were gone, the militias had come and looted everything in the house. Even the Somali flag was gone, lying in the dust in the street, torn through with bullet holes.

Three hours later, Siciid's black truck, stuffed with belongings, kids, and women, appeared at the house. Dad was sitting on the back side of the truck and was so covered with dust I could hardly recognize his face.

We squeezed in, Mom crouching, holding Nima and me, Dad holding Hassan. We were off to Baidoa.

But after about five hundred yards, a group of rebels blocked the truck, ordering us to stop. One wavy-haired, thin, and dark man pointed his gun at Siciid. His accent was from Galgaduud region; he talked fast and looked sideways with the gun on Siciid's head. Three others pulled things out of the back: the mattresses, Dad's basketball medals,

Mom's necklace of black wenge beads. My parents just watched as everything they had worked for was destroyed.

"Who are you people? What is your clan?" asked a gunman.

"We are Rahanweyn," said Mom. I hoped they would let us go.

"Come out of the truck, all of you!"

Under her shawl, Mom concealed her bag, which contained money and almost everything else my family had left.

"What is under your garment?" he demanded.

"Cosmetics," said Mom.

"Give it to me!" he yelled, holding his gun to my head. Mostly, I was scared by how tight the gunman was holding me and how skinny his legs were. And because I was just a little boy, what also scared me was seeing my mom cry. Never had I seen her cry so hard. He took the money from her bag, threw it aside, and with a shake of his gun yelled, "Be gone!"

• • •

With nothing left for anyone to steal, we continued driving through Mogadishu. The road was crowded, and all of the traffic was in one direction: out of the city. Parked at the side of the road at intervals were more pickup trucks with teenagers dressed in tattered vests, sitting in the beds, chewing qat leaves and pointing guns at the vehicles passing by. These were militias of the Hawiye clan loyal to Aidid. They were killing anyone they could find who was loyal to the government or a member of the Darod clan.

Sometimes I saw them laughing, or pointing their guns at each other and yelling in unfamiliar accents. It was like a game to them.

As we continued, I saw more vehicles being stopped by the militias. I saw someone on the ground being kicked; then I saw a corpse, piles of corpses. Nearby, I saw a line of about twenty people standing, awaiting execution. I peeped my head out of the truck to watch militiamen pushing more people to the line; then, to our horror, two skinny men shot them all. Yet their terrible fate was our good luck: the rebels were too busy shooting them to stop my family, and we moved on. My mom murmured passages from the Koran.

Eventually, we were stopped at another checkpoint manned by about a hundred militiamen, as Siciid lurched to a stop. They came from all directions, running toward us and climbing onto the back. Nima was crying, Hassan tried to hide behind the jerry can of water, I ducked my head. They dragged Dad and Siciid out of the truck and pushed them facedown in the sand. My dad's dark sunglasses were beside him; a rebel stooped and picked them up, blew the dust off the lenses, and put them on his thin face. He showed his militia friends and smiled.

Dad looked toward us, widening his eyes and giving a small nod of his head to tell us to stay calm. The guy who took the sunglasses saw my dad's watch and jerked it from his wrist. Meanwhile, a middle-aged woman jumped onto our truck to mug us, but she couldn't find anything to steal. "You just poor people," she said with a sour face, and slipped away from the truck, disappointed.

One of the younger fighters, who looked about sixteen, held his gun to Siciid's head. "Let's kill them."

"No," said an older man. "Our fight is with the Darod clan."

They grabbed Dad and Siciid and started to drag them away. Dad whispered, "Don't worry, I'll be fine." After twenty minutes under the hot sun, the militiamen told us to go, but first they emptied the truck of the rest of our few possessions. Dad and Siciid appeared from an alley and were kicked roughly toward the truck by rebels. They had been beaten badly.

As Siciid drove us away, Mom sobbed. "Next time we won't make it! We will all die! I'm scared for the children. Turn around!"

"We'll make it to Baidoa if Allah wills," said Dad, "so stay calm." Mom continued reciting the Koran with a loud voice and kept telling us that with her reciting we would be fine. She was wishing she had never lived in Mogadishu. *We should have stayed in the bush. Better to contend with the drought and the wild animals than this.*

Miles out of Mogadishu, there were no more roadblocks, just blowing sand and thornbushes. We turned off onto a dirt track and reached a bank of greenery—mango trees, banana palms, watermelon, and long grass—as the road reached a river. A troop of blue monkeys descended from the trees onto the truck, looking for food. Of course we had none. Their silver faces and blank orange eyes terrified me.

We reached the edge of the town of Afgooye. Siciid stopped the truck along the roadside for us to relieve ourselves. My mom accompanied Hassan and me down near the river. As I peed, I kept looking around for monkeys that might snatch me from the ground and eat me. Nearby, I saw a woman celebrating the fall of the government, dressed in black and with her head covered; she chattered as we peed. She claimed we were on her land and said we may not eat her crops. The land was full of ripe mangoes, bananas, and fat round watermelons. I grabbed Mom, and as she looked down with her worn face, I touched my belly to show her I was hungry. She said she could not do anything, but she fetched some water from the muddy river. It seemed dirty to me, but I was thirsty, so I drank until my belly filled up.

Back on the road, the scorching sun cooled slowly as it slipped beneath the dusty horizon. It was not long before our truck reached another checkpoint. A group of soldiers wearing government military uniforms stopped the car. They wore the badge of the government's Supreme Revolutionary Council, with President Siad Barre's image. So they were not rebels! Dad jumped down confidently to meet them. War songs blasted out of their cars, with lyrics encouraging the soldiers not to give up, to fight and recapture Mogadishu.

"We are displaced to Baidoa by the rebels," Dad said. The soldiers waved him back into the truck to continue the journey.

After another half an hour, we saw a military vehicle blocking the road ahead—another checkpoint by soldiers loyal to President Siad Barre, with their flag still flying. "These soldiers are the Marehan," Siciid murmured to

Mom. She knew what that meant: The Marehan were the same tribe of the Darod clan as the president, but they were not regular army like the last soldiers we saw. They didn't care about the government; they were just seeking revenge against the tribes who kicked them out of the city. There were so many sides in this war, and I was too young to understand it.

Siciid turned the truck suddenly, and guns aimed at us from all directions. A bullet shattered the wing mirror close to me, almost deafening my left ear. Siciid stopped the truck. Dad remained motionless, hiding in the back of the truck.

A soldier looked at us. "Who are you?"

"We are a poor family," Mom pleaded. "We are displaced to Baidoa by the fighting."

"Where is your husband?" the soldier asked.

"Asalaamu aleikum!"—Peace be upon you! It was my dad's voice, brave as always. "These are my kids and wife; I am taking them to the safety of the bush." But before he finished what he wanted to say, the butt of a gun smashed into his head. The skinny militiamen continued to beat him. I watched in despair as my tall, strong, proud dad was brought to his knees.

Then a voice called out from the group of fighters. "Nur Dhere!"—Tall Nur! A man ran over to Dad. In joy they shook hands and hugged each other.

"Ahmed, Ahmed!" Dad said, recognizing the man. Ahmed was a traffic officer from Mogadishu and a friend of my dad's. He was as tall as Dad, with thick glasses and a large mustache. They started talking about their time during the peace together and remembering the games Ahmed attended, games that Dad won for the national team. Ahmed thanked Dad for a time when my dad gave him money. The soldiers, noticing this exchange, let us go and turned to the truck behind us while Dad chatted with his friend. For a moment we felt safe and unharmed, but we could hear the cries of the women being beaten in the next truck and couldn't help but imagine it happening to us.

Siciid joined the two of them and Ahmed reached into his pocket for a cigarette to share. Ahmed kept talking to my dad and Siciid while his fellow soldiers shot and beat families in the trucks behind us. Whenever the soldiers fired, I flinched and ducked behind my mom. My poor mom watched with her hand on her head.

After a few minutes they said good-bye and we left, amazed at our own good luck. What would have happened if Dad hadn't been recognized? Mom's face shone wet with tears of joy. "We've survived again!" she cried to Siciid when we sped off. "We have another day to live!"

■ ■ ■

The only noises I could hear, apart from the humming of the truck's engine, were the braying of donkeys, the moos of cows, the bleats of goats, and the bells around the necks of camels. Our headlights revealed houses made of sticks and dung, between which was just enough room for the truck to squeeze by. Dad walked in front of the truck now, moving branches to the side of the track. Mom sniffed the air and said, "I swear this is Baidoa." She started humming songs for her animals, she was so excited to be home.

"Aeeyy! Aeeyy! Aeeyy!" came a strange sound. I was afraid, but Dad, Mom, and Siciid were not startled. I realized it was being made by herdsmen leading their camels into a corral. An old man with a long stick appeared behind the truck and walked slowly along the side. Dad caught up with him. The old man kept saying *"Aeeyy!"* as he chatted with Dad in the Maay dialect. Thankfully, the man followed nomad custom by feeding us all with the fresh milk from his camel. We were so hungry. Mom, Siciid, and Dad helped with the milking. Hassan and I watched the camel's face in wonder. We had never been so close to a camel. Its neck seemed too large to be real, and it was chewing something, its fuzzy lips moving back and forth against crooked amber teeth.

The truck was almost out of gas, said Siciid, and there was no gas anywhere to buy, even if we had money. We lumbered up to a fence built of thorns. Dad got out and knocked at the fence post repeatedly, but there was no reply. Finally he stepped back, ran hard like he was making a layup shot, and jumped over.

"Who are you?" came a deep voice in Maay, from inside the wall.

"It is me, Nur," said Dad.

"Allah be praised! Where have you come from on this dark night?"

As the gate of thorns swung open, I was surprised to see that the voice belonged to a woman. It was Aseey, my dad's aunt. She was tall and strong, gap-toothed. She was holding on to a big stick because she said the lion Fareey's pride was still active at night. She hugged us all. Soon we were cross-legged and devouring white maize with beans. She said the Somali Patriotic Movement, a group of Darod tribesmen led by Omar Jess—a rebel from the Siad Barre government—were on their way to attack Baidoa. They wanted possession of the fertile lands around the city in central Somalia. These militiamen were once loyal soldiers of the Somali government but had formed their own faction. Most men were fleeing the city, because they were the main targets. Women feared rape. For the first time, my parents understood that the conflict they thought existed only in Mogadishu was in fact everywhere. They didn't know where to go from Baidoa.

Dad rose to his feet, smiling, but there was fear in his eyes. "If we wait until morning, all the roads out of Baidoa will be blocked and there will be no escape. Siciid and I must leave straightaway. Don't worry, we're all going to be okay." Dad was leaving to save us. He knew his presence with us could kill us all, because the militias were terminating men with their families all together. But they might spare kids with moms. The close calls we had on our trip from Mogadishu were enough to explain what would happen.

Dad and Siciid talked about what to do. Dad knew the bushlands well and Siciid knew the roads, a good combination. But they decided it was best to split up when they got out of town, making it harder to see them. They would walk into the bush, away from the gunfire. That was their only plan. Dad kissed each of us on the forehead, then left, pausing outside the gate to wave and force a smile. He re-turned in a second to grab a stick to fend off hyenas and lions, then walked out and down the road with Siciid, past the truck and its empty gas tank. I watched my tall dad dis-appear into the dark night.

· 3 ·

TRAIL OF THORNS

We were four, with no dad. Five if you counted the baby inside Mom. Just me, Hassan, Nima, and pregnant Mom. That night I heard gunfire. Every shot worried us it might be Dad. Mom and Aunt Aseey were reading the Koran. The gunfire continued all night. Mom told us we would leave in the morning by foot into the bush; I knew from her stories that we could face wild animals, thirst, and hunger.

As the sun was rising, we crept through the thorn fence, trembling while listening to the sounds of war. Finally a bazooka shell hit the fence in a fiery explosion. There were gunmen nearby. We could not stay here. I was six years old and learning that nowhere in the world was safe.

Twilight. Mom tied Nima to her back and grabbed me and Hassan by the arms. Aseey paced around for a minute and decided to leave by herself. We said goodbye to her and headed out into the darkening streets.

Mom led with Nima on her shoulders, me and Hassan behind in bare feet—we never owned shoes, even before the war. In front of us, we saw a horrifying sight: dogs chewing on dead bodies. Then more bullets arcing through the night, and flashes of light, and from time to time, we heard women screaming. Mom had known these narrow alleyways since her childhood, so she found hiding places by the side of the huts whenever we saw or heard any movement.

At the edge of the town, we looked back and saw that much of Baidoa was burning. In front of us was the bush, that dangerous land of lions and hyenas. She pointed out places where she'd chased hyenas and herded goats in her childhood, but this time I was not ready to hear any stories; I was struggling to stay on my feet.

The bush hid us from gunmen. Instead, we contended with the vultures and crows that were swarming everywhere. Mom angrily shooed them away. We carried on in silence, even though the cuts from the thornbushes made us want to scream. The ride with Dad and Siciid in the truck now seemed so much better. Mom was used to the bush, but we were not. Overwhelmed by hunger, thirst, and fatigue, I was by now being pulled along by Mom until finally I fell. Hassan sat down beside me. His lips were cracking. Mom looked back and remarked that she no longer saw fires or heard bullets. "There may be predators and snakes here, but we are safe from the soldiers," she said. "We'll sleep under this acacia tree."

Mom tried to stay awake to guard us, but she was too desperately tired. Soon we were all asleep.

When the sun woke Mom, she stood up quickly. "Look at all the footprints of animals, so many of them! Let's go before they return." Strange sounds filled the land, sounds I'd never heard in Mogadishu. I couldn't tell if they were birds or animals, but Mom could tell. She even knew if the sound was a female or a male. She looked, smelled, listened, and then knew which way to go. I was grateful she was so knowledgeable.

We continued walking through the heat. I had stomach pains and my feet were bleeding, but Mom knew what to do. She went off for a few minutes, then returned with some leaves in her hand. These are the *awrodhaye* plants, she said, good for wounds. We watched her chew the leaves, then put the paste on our stinging feet like an ointment. It felt so good. I always thought her nomad stories were like fairy tales; they seemed so far away from our city life in Mogadishu. But we were living them, and I saw how much my mom really knew about how to survive. And now, without Dad to lead us, I saw how strong and brave she was. At that moment in the bush, I vowed that I would always survive like her.

Suddenly, Mom stooped low, waving her hand downward to tell us to do the same. A group of five militiamen. We heard them yelling in Maay dialect. "They are Rahanweyn! Thank Allah!" Mom stood and walked toward them. "How are you?" she shouted in Maay.

All five of the Rahanweyn men looked to be in their thirties, dressed in tattered shirts. They listened to Mom's account of our escape. "There is no possibility that you can escape this way because you are heading toward their territory," one of the men said. "You will stand a better chance in Baidoa."

But we already knew we could not go back to Baidoa, and wondered if any place was safe.

By now my stomach pains had turned into diarrhea from dehydration; Hassan wasn't much better, so we needed to stop a lot. Mom made us chew the *awrodhaye*; it was bitter and sour but still comforting. Finally we reached the main road to Mogadishu, where we flagged down a truck so crowded with people that it was standing room only in the back. The truck was going to Mogadishu, from where we had fled only days before. What else could we do? We had no more strength to walk through the bush, and no food or water. But the road back to Mogadishu was not the same as two days earlier. Power had shifted into the hands of General Aidid's USC militias, and the violence was everywhere. We saw that the mango trees in Afgooye had all been destroyed. Even the crocodiles and monkeys were dead. Militias hid in the bushes, ambushing people and raping women.

We rode in a banana truck. Everyone was trying to find a banana to scavenge, but there were none left. The luckiest ones found a few banana peels and ate those. Mom found none for us. She didn't bother to complain that she was pregnant; no one could afford to help anyone else.

The road was blocked with boulders and burning cars, and the driver threaded the truck through the debris. In order to move forward, he jumped out and kicked dead bodies out of the roadway. We drove on for more than 120 miles. My stomach throbbed. I was barely conscious, aware of the flies, the heat, and the pain, and of Mom's trembling hand holding on to my own. I was aware of the checkpoint that the truck was approaching and of the gunshots that hit the vehicle, but by now I was prepared to accept any outcome. Even death.

Then I was aware of the driver on the ground, pleading with the gunmen. He was of the Darod clan like them, he explained desperately, and was taking sick people to Mogadishu. He offered the gunmen money. I was aware of harsh, merciless faces looking at him, aware of the dirt and smell of them. You can't know what clan or tribe someone belongs to just by looking at them. You can tell only by their speech, so people learned how to fake accents. Maybe the driver was pretending to be Darod to appease them; I didn't know. But my mom could fake any accent; she was prepared for anything.

I realized that the vehicle was moving again and that it had turned off the road to avoid more checkpoints or militias. But then, less than twelve miles from Mogadishu, a bullet shattered the side window and exploded in the driver's head. The truck veered wildly off the road, then shuddered into a ditch and finally stopped at a sharp angle. Everyone panicked and stumbled out of the back of the truck, pushing and shoving. A woman threw me off the truck and I landed on the ground. Mom struggled to keep us together, holding Nima tight. I took one last look at the truck and at the driver who moments earlier was kicking dead bodies off the road, now himself dead.

Mom knew we too might die any minute and she was thinking our dad was dead by now, but she said she would die herself before she left our bodies to rot on the road. The rebels who shot the driver ran toward the truck. Mom took our hands, me and Hassan, Nima on her back, and we walked again into the blazing bush. With our brave mom by our side, we would live or die in Mogadishu.

CITY OF WOMEN AND CHILDREN

Many Somalis made it to North America and Europe, where they found a better life. And then there were people like us, mostly women and children, returning to Mogadishu because we had no other place to go. We were trapped.

Mogadishu had become a city of graves. The streets were littered with bullet casings. Exhausted militiamen roamed the empty neighborhoods, carrying the goods they looted going from house to house. The great capital city of the nation had become the valley of death.

We stood there—Hassan, me, my pregnant mom with Nima on her back, and no dad—all of us dazed. We could not believe what guns could do to a whole city. And the smell. Blood has a smell, metallic and musty like the smell of coins in a dirty pocket, and you can smell it when it covers the streets and turns rusty in the dust. That and the rank odor of smoldering buildings.

With my brother and me trailing behind Mom, we passed the bombed-out Cinema Ecuatore, the ruins of restaurants and clubs. There were no more signs for comedy shows. There was nothing to laugh about. We finally got to our house. It was a ruin. Rockets had pierced jagged holes in all sides of our rooms. Gone was the furniture my parents had proudly bought with Dad's basketball earnings. Gone were the wooden window shutters, or any windows you might shut. Gone were the shelves. Rebel soldiers had been using what was left of the rooms as an outhouse, and there were stinking piles of feces swarming with flies everywhere. The neem tree was still standing, covered in dust.

Hassan and I were so glad to be home; we did not care about the mess. But Mom said no. "We cannot stay here," she said.

Our bare feet were bleeding from running on the rough ground in the baking sun. In our search for a place to stay that night, all we could see were people ducking from gunfire as they crossed the streets. Sometimes we would catch up with another confused family, a mom and kids like us, and together we would sit on the side of the road. It felt so good to sit after a long walk. Hassan removed tiny stones from my feet as I lay on my back.

Soon it was dark. With no electricity, the city became pitch-black. Mom was still trying to find us a place to spend the night. She had one place in mind: under the KM4 Street bridge. It was a few miles' walk, but when we got there, Mom was right: it seemed quieter in the dark tunnel. We heard only the distant gunshots and the soft wind of the night. Mom spread her scarf on the dusty road. We were all so tired. Hassan and I rested our heads on the scarf; Mom cuddled Nima. The waves of the ocean, the cool breeze, and the chirping crickets sent me into a deep sleep.

But that tunnel turned out to be not so quiet. Our sleep was interrupted by dogs that growled as they scavenged. Finally, at dawn, I opened my eyes to see Mom and Hassan standing in the tunnel crying, *"Lailaha ilallah!"*—There is no god but Allah. They were standing on top of a graveyard. We had not noticed at night, but now we saw the place we had slept was where bodies had been hastily buried beneath a thin layer of dirt. These corpses weren't even rotting yet. We saw dogs tugging at bare feet. There was flesh everywhere. It looked like roadkill on highways. We fled again, retching from the scene.

For weeks we slept on the streets with the dead. Mom would sing the lullaby "Huwaaya Huwaa" in her weak voice, but with our empty bellies, the song was not sending us to sleep. We got used to the corpses, but we could not get used to our painfully empty stomachs. After days of no food or water, we ate whatever we could chew—unripe neem tree fruit that tasted like bitter olives, lizards we could catch. Nothing was too disgusting, even dead skin we peeled off our feet. We were sick with dysentery and dehydration. As many people were dying from disease as from bullets.

When Nima cried for milk, Mom tried to breastfeed her, but no milk came out. Our little sister was shrinking from malnourishment.

Meanwhile, Mom's belly was growing big with her baby. The bugs sucked blood from her skin, and she scratched every second. Mom was scared for the labor. The baby would come soon. Bad timing—our newest sibling was on the way to hell on earth. No one expected this baby to make it.

Khadija Ahmed was the only neighbor we could recognize still remaining in the city. Her family had remained in Mogadishu, but her husband had been killed in their house just a few days earlier; the family was in mourning when we arrived. We met Khadija as she was clearing some rubble on the street. Mom and Khadija hugged, surprised to see each other alive. Khadija had three living kids, a boy named Abdikadir, who was almost my age, and two teenage daughters, Fatuma and Fardowsa. Another son, Kaafi, had been killed.

Khadija decided to take us in. She had given us some water and porridge, but none of us could swallow the food; we were too dehydrated. My soul wanted the food but my body could not yet handle it. It was a big relief to finally be able to sleep in a room. The walls were made of cardboard, but at least the dry dust off the streets was no longer hitting our faces. Every night before we went to bed, we sat quietly in a circle under the dark sky of Mogadishu with the stars blinking, gazing up at them. Somalis believe each star represents a person who died. I looked at the brightest star and imagined my dad winking at me from heaven.

•••

When the militias of the Hawiye clan entered Mogadishu and deposed President Siad Barre, they were united in that cause. But in late 1991, once Siad Barre had been defeated and the government destroyed, the Hawiye splintered into two tribes, the Abgaal and the Habargidir, and they began fighting each other for control of the city. This was the second phase of the civil war, known as the Four-Month War. This fight would turn out to be even worse, because by now, there were so many weapons in Mogadishu. It would end in the total destruction of the city, and it began just as we arrived at Khadija's house.

Mom and Khadija were out every day clearing bodies from the streets, trying to bury them properly. This was for both respect and sanitation. Hassan and I slowly recovered from our dehydration and were able to eat a little porridge. I became good friends with Khadija's son Abdikadir. We played war games, making AK-47 rifles out of tree branches and shooting at each other. We could make very realistic gun sounds with our mouths, because we were hearing real guns all around us every day. We cheered each other on, imagining violent scenarios. In this way we coped with our deep and constant fear and insecurity. Together with Hassan and Khadija's girls, we also played hide-and-seek in the empty houses surrounding us, jumping from window to window. Whenever a house was blasted, we would run to it and hope to find new hiding spots.

But the porridge soon ran out, and we had to scavenge in the streets for any food. We became so weak that we spoke in whispers, unable to vocalize. Every evening, Mom and Khadija would return with so much worry on their faces. By now the militias were fighting in every corner of the city, trying to take control block by block. The constant roar of their rocket-propelled grenade launchers and automatic machine guns almost deafened us. Abdikadir and I looked through the bullet holes in our walls, watching the action. All we could smell was gunpowder and blood. Our only toys were the bullet casings that littered the street. We learned how to count using those shells, and we learned to identify which guns had fired them.

As the war continued, soon came a new misery: the first drought since the one in 1977 that had forced my parents out of the nomad life and into the city. The 1992 drought was even worse. All my grandparents survived the drought of 1977, but they could not survive this one. Only later did we learn that they died, all four of them, after all their remaining animals were wiped out and they could not find water or food. Their wealth, their bravery, and their pride were gone. The Iftin family that once boasted of hundreds of animals had vanished from the earth as if in an apocalypse.

...

Khadija called us orphans because we had no dad. Now we had another orphan in our family. My new baby sister was born during the Four-Month War. Khadija helped Mom deliver in the middle of the night using a flashlight, while Hassan and I waited outside the room, curious. Amazingly, the baby came out breathing and healthy. Unlike when I was born, Mom did not have people visit, or bring herbs, food, and clothes. There was no rest for forty days. The day after Sadia was born, Mom was forced to go out and find food for us.

My strong mom was getting weaker, and she was no longer the beautiful nomad girl whom my dad had fallen for. Swollen feet, hunger, sleepless nights with the baby, and constant worry had beaten her down. Madinah Ibrahim Moalim, brave daughter of her brave parents, was giving up the fight. She could no longer care for us. My brother and I, now eight and seven, knew that if our family was to have water and food, we would need to get it ourselves. Our mom had kept us alive this far; now we needed to keep our sisters and her alive. They needed us. And so we put aside our games of hide-and-seek and our bullet-casing toys and got to work.

The only place to get water in our quarter of Mogadishu was the well pump at Madinah Hospital, three miles distant along a road lined with sniper posts. This was the same hospital next to Dad's cousin Mumin's house where we had spent the night when the civil war broke out. Now it was a ruin. Hassan and I hauled our twenty-liter jerry can over to fill up with water. When we arrived, the line for the water tap was hours long, in the glaring sun. The rebels who controlled Madinah were not as bad as the street militias. They minded their own business while we filled up our cans. We would put the can in the line and then try to sit in the shade of a tree, keeping a close eye on that can so no one would cut ahead of us. It felt so good when our turn came and we finally had fresh water. The can weighed forty-four pounds full, but it was cylindrical, so we could roll it home, especially since the road that way was downhill. As we kicked and rolled that jerry can and ran, we crouched to avoid being seen by the snipers. The bullets that hit the wall above our heads sent dust into our ears.

One morning we woke to the usual sound of gunfire but also to the voice of a man in the house. He wasn't yelling like a fighter. Who was this male visitor in the city of women and children? We rose and saw to our dismay that it was Macalin Basbaas, the neighborhood Koranic scholar. He was back from the bush and ready to reopen his madrassa. He led us all—Mom, Khadija, Hassan, and me—in a long prayer. With that, Hassan and I as well as Khadija's kids had been signed up for the madrassa. War or no war, learning the Koran must go on. Lessons would start immediately, and we left with Macalin Basbaas for his mud-walled school.

There were only ten students, including us, at the school, all of us sitting on the dirt with our wooden writing boards on our laps. From that day on, on top of war, thirst, and hunger, we bore the daily beating of Macalin Basbaas and his hard sticks. Any mistake in our lessons, which consisted entirely of memorizing the Koran in Arabic rather than our native tongue, was an excuse for a serious beating. Each day I memorized several verses of the Koran by heart. The first few chapters are short, and they are mostly verses I had learned at home from Mom. But each day that passed, they grew longer and harder to memorize, and the flogging doubled each time we made a mistake. I felt I needed magic to carry them all in my head.

Every evening, we returned home bleeding and wounded from the brutal, endless whippings. The teacher's cruelty was not unusual or personal; all madrassas relied on corporal punishment. In fact, parents expected it as part of a rigorous education. When we got home, sometimes I could not open my mouth to describe my pain, but all Mom could see was that her sons were learning all 114 chapters of the Koran. We had missed so much school because of the war, and now was our chance to catch up on memorizing God's holy word, to learn discipline and mental strength. I was angry and felt betrayed, but the madrassa was the only type of education available to us. In those terrible times, sending us to school was Mom's way of looking out for us.

• • •

In early 1992, the Four-Month War ended in a stalemate with no winner. Exhausted militiamen, still holding guns, sat in the beds of their pickup trucks (known as "technicals"), on every corner of the city. Most of these rebels were loyal to Mohamed Farrah Aidid. Aidid's rebel organization, the USC, controlled twelve of the sixteen districts of Mogadishu. The rest, mainly in the north of the city, were controlled by the warlord Ali Mahdi. Between Mahdi's forces and Aidid's forces, "green lines" were established that divided the city. Meanwhile, Aidid moved deep into inland Somalia with his soldiers, grabbing land and killing anyone armed who was not on his side. One of the places Aidid seized was Baidoa. When Aidid and his militias entered the town, they met the dying and starving faces of the Rahanweyn; the drought had hit hard in this area. Aidid's militias remained in town for the next two years until the locals armed themselves and pushed back against them.

The famine drove many from Baidoa and other areas into Mogadishu. They arrived by foot, thousands every day. The streets were filled with women and children begging and dying, very thin and ill. Many headed straight to Madinah Hospital for water. The lines at the single pump got longer and longer, hundreds of people.

Meanwhile, the stalemate did not mean the fighting stopped; it just became unpredictable. Usually the opposing sides would send up their rockets and shells at night. We heard them exploding around the neighborhood as we cowered in our beds, hoping we would not be among the unlucky ones who got hit.

I could recognize some of the faces among the newly returned, people I had known in the city before the war. I saw the same kids who used to bully me, jealous that my dad was a basketball star; now they were back with their uncles who were in the militias. Now they bullied all of us. Hassan, who once put them in their place, now had to stand there and take it as they beat him. If we fought them, we would surely be killed by their uncles. So we were bullied every single day. This was the new order of Mogadishu. Families harassed other families. Guns ruled the city. There were no laws, no rules; justice did not exist.

Our Rahanweyn clan had always been stigmatized by the more powerful Hawiye. Now, in the lawless city, we were threatened every day. Clan became the only thing people talked about. Hassan and I started to speak only in the Mogadishu accent, to disguise what tribe we belonged to. We would even lie and say we were Hawiye. Our mom had used the same tactic to save our lives during the flight from Mogadishu. So we were learning from her how to survive. But she was a nomad from the bush. Hassan and I were born in Mogadishu, and we felt like guests in our own city. People who had never set foot in Mogadishu before the war were ruling the streets.

When we weren't carrying water or attending the madrassa, Hassan and I roamed the streets in search of food for our family. Everyone in Mogadishu said the same thing: "Eat anything that does not eat you." It felt like all the curses of the universe had descended upon us. First war, then natural disaster, then disease. There were no working hospitals, no clinics or medicine to treat illness. All became things you just had to live with, or die from. Mogadishu had become a city of walking skeletons, everyone thin and malnourished. Somalis called it *Caga Bararki,* "the time of swollen feet." Everybody's feet had blown up like balloons due to severe malnourishment and fluid retention. It became hard to walk, but we had to walk to get water. So our mom used cactus thorns to pierce and drain our feet.

Our newborn sister, Sadia, was not even able to sit up. She was so tiny and thin, struggling to breathe. Nothing helped. Khadija was often in the room with Mom, discussing what they could do to save the baby. Finally, there was only prayer.

The day my baby sister died, Hassan and I dug the grave for her in the front yard of Khadija's house. I looked at her and kissed her on the forehead. We wrapped her in a small white scarf and laid her in her tiny grave before sunset. Hassan and I shared the news of her death with friends and people in the neighborhood, but no one expressed sorrow or even cared. Death was everywhere; it was not a big deal. It was nothing to talk about. After a few prayers, we got on with our own survival.

Lucky for our sister, she had left the cruel world of guns and bloodshed. She was now in heaven eating sweet ripe fruit and floating on a river of milk and honey guarded by the angels. Or so we were told. The rest of us trudged on with our daily struggles. Mom prayed and read the Koran for another day of survival. The stories Mom told us about heaven, life after death, and the privilege of being a Muslim child encouraged us to not fear the end. Mom talked about the rivers of milk and honey, the beautiful endless good life in heaven. No wars, no bullying. It made us feel guilty for living in the hell on earth, like we had done something bad to deserve it. So we prayed.

· 5 ·

ARABIC TO ENGLISH

By late 1992, rain had finally come to Somalia. People were selling food on the street—small piles of tomatoes, bundles of sugarcane, ears of corn—which they had brought in from the countryside. We desperately needed coins to buy food, so Hassan and I hatched a plan to make money: selling water. At this point we had two twenty-liter jerry cans, so we could split up. I would get water for our family with one can. With the other, Hassan would find people willing to pay him to get water for them—especially if they were too afraid to go through the city and risk passing by the snipers. Hassan learned he could move faster and earn more money by carrying his water can on his back. But eventually this caused him so much back and shoulder pain that he screamed in agony every night. We needed another plan.

The militiamen were all addicted to qat, which they

chewed constantly and which energized them to fight. The qat came into Mogadishu by boat and by land, a lot of it from Kenya. Hassan and I would sneak behind them and collect any leaves they dropped, which we could then re-sell. We joined a group of other kids who also roamed the streets day and night finding loose qat. Sometimes we even stole leaves from delivery trucks. Many times the butt of a gun would hit me and send me tumbling off the moving truck empty-handed. But other times I ended up with some fresh leaves that I could sell on the streets.

It felt like bringing a medal home as we walked into the house with maize, milk, and fruits for our family, paid for with our qat money. Mom cooked the maize, put it in a bowl, and added milk. Hassan, Nima, and I sat in a circle surrounding the bowl. Mom would not eat until we were full. She always ate just the little that stuck to the bottom of the pot, scraping every last bit of it out.

While Hassan and I were out, Nima stayed behind. She mostly spent her days outside the house, in a deep melancholy. Sometimes she sat right on top of Sadia's grave with her cheek on the sand, like she was communicating with our dead sister. When Hassan and I arrived home, Nima would run and hug us. In the conservative Somali culture, girls never associate with men, even their own brothers, but Hassan and I refused to accept that. She was not going to the madrassa, but we taught her the basics of the Koran by reading to her in Arabic, and she picked up some verses.

• • •

With so much of the city destroyed, people moved into houses whose owners had either died or never returned. Old buildings of universities, schools, and hospitals became makeshift refugee camps. But some people also returned to their former houses, including a woman named Falis who would change my life.

Falis was a tall, dark woman in her twenties. Like many sophisticated Mogadishu women, she wore makeup— including eyeliner and a bright yellow foundation made from ground turmeric. In peacetime she had been fat, which in Somalia is a sign of beauty. Many men chased her. But during the war, she came back thin, and she was worried that her beauty was gone. She had been lucky that her house survived the war, in part thanks to having relatives in the militias who guarded it while she was gone. Before the war, Falis sold movie tickets at the Cinema Ecuatore; she remembered seeing my dad there with his friends in those peaceful days. When she came back to Mogadishu, she was able to get a television, some videocassettes, and a VCR, which she set up in a shack attached to her house. She started a makeshift cinema and dance parlor, hoping to charge a few coins for admission. At first she wouldn't let us kids wander in, but we would listen outside her door. One of the tapes she played over and over was the Michael Jackson music video *Thriller*, and I would dance with other boys to the beat in her courtyard. I loved that song so much.

One day when I was out there dancing, Falis came out to hang movie posters of Rambo, the Terminator, and Chuck Norris. I stared at the men in the posters—big strong

Americans, flexing huge muscles, not like the skinny people in Mogadishu. I didn't understand what an actor was, or that Rambo, the Terminator, and Commando were characters. I just went and looked at those posters every day, imagining what those strong people must be like. Sometimes rebels would come up to the posters and spit on them, like they were picking a fight with the men. Whoever these men were, I knew it would be a fight the rebels could never win. The weapons the movie people carried were much bigger and shinier than anything the militias had in Mogadishu.

Falis needed help getting that shack cleaned up and ready for people to watch the movies. Because I was always hanging around, looking at the posters or dancing, she asked if I would help. For the first time, I was allowed inside. The shack had a dirt floor and was filthy. I got to work, climbing up into narrow corners and pulling off spiderwebs, dusting off the TV screen, cleaning the cassettes, fetching water, and arranging where people would sit. Finally the space was ready. I was so excited that I was going to see the people on those posters in a movie!

The first movie Hassan and I saw was *Commando*, starring Arnold Schwarzenegger. I sat with my jaw practically on the dirt floor, my eyes popping out. The audience cheered, laughed, and applauded whenever an action scene happened. Of course none of us knew any English and we couldn't understand anything they were saying, so whenever there was dialogue, we shouted at Commando to stop talking and shoot to kill. Everyone hated the talk; they wanted bloodshed, just like life in Mogadishu, but better.

I loved the action, but I also had a burning desire to know what they were saying. So, glued to the screen, I watched the actors intensely as they talked, trying to read their lips. I picked up phrases that were repeated often, most of them related to guns and death. I realized I had some ability to hear the words easily and remember them.

Falis let Hassan and me watch the movies in return for sweeping the dirt floor. Whenever we weren't at the madrassa or fetching food and water, we were there. We saw *Rambo,* and *The Terminator,* and *The Delta Force.* All action movies. I got to know the scenes by heart, exactly what would happen and what Commando or the Terminator or Rambo would say. I met new friends in the movie shack, Mohammed, Bashi, and Bocow. At the end of the day, when Falis said she was closing, we would walk home and quiz each other on the movie, discussing what we liked. We would act out scenes, throwing rocks, jumping over debris, and pretending to speak English. I read Arnold's lips and moved my mouth the way he did. I drove my mom crazy saying "I'll be back!" over and over again. I didn't even know what it meant, but I knew it sounded cool.

For the first time in years, since going with my dad to the basketball games, I felt truly happy. My strong dad was gone, but now I had these big strong action heroes to look up to. I wanted Commando to come to Mogadishu and kill all the militias in the city.

Hassan and I still had to feed our family. How could we go to the movies and make money at the same time? We hit on the idea of selling popcorn and peanuts in the video shack. We didn't even know Americans buy popcorn when they go to movies; this was just an idea we had. We borrowed raw peanuts in the shell from a market lady, who agreed to the loan when we told her our plan and promised we could pay her back. We got some corn kernels the same way. Hassan and I shelled the peanuts and roasted them over a fire at home. We popped the corn in a kettle of our mom's. Then we carried the snacks, still warm, to the video shack and sold it all. Even Falis bought some. We were able to pay back the market women, buy food for our family, and watch a movie.

The movie shack became a second home to me, and Falis became like family. I even started calling her aunt. Hassan and I started skipping the madrassa to go to the movies and sell peanuts and popcorn. Of course, we never told Mom. She thought movies were evil and not a place for good Muslims. But we weren't alone. Many students were skipping the madrassa to watch the movies. One day, Macalin Basbaas showed up at the video shack and found five of us watching *Commando* when we should have been in school. He dragged us out and marched us back to the school in a rage. He beat me until my body was covered in blood. I tried to be strong like Sylvester Stallone in *Rambo*, but it was hard in real life and I screamed for help. Macalin Basbaas's hard sticks on my skin seemed even worse than bullets.

Soon enough, I was going back to the movies; even beatings couldn't keep me away. In those movies, I learned about life beyond Somalia and Islam. I had never seen a map of the world. I didn't know the difference between Europe and America. I had no knowledge of geography or history, only what Macalin Basbaas had taught us in Arabic about Islam, Saudi Arabia, and Egypt. But in the movies, I saw brave soldiers and beautiful women. There were no ruins, the streets were clean and nice; the wars were always fought somewhere else. There was lots of food. I thought, "Whoever these people are, they are great!" I prayed to Allah that someday I could meet some of these strange foreigners.

• • •

By December 1992, the world could no longer sit back while Somalia was starving. Humanitarian aid had been coming into Somalia for months, but the warlords would hoard all the food and medicine donations for themselves. Finally the United Nations decided to take action. Led by the United States, twenty-eight countries organized a military task force called Operation Restore Hope. The goal was to supervise the distribution of food and supplies to the Somalian people.

In Somalia we call Americans *Mareekans*. When I heard these *Mareekans* were coming to Mogadishu, I asked my mom who they were. I didn't know the people in the action movies were *Mareekans*. "They are huge, strong white people," she said. "They eat pork, drink wine, and have dogs in their houses."

This sounded like the people I had seen in the movies. Whoever they were, the militiamen looked worried about their arrival. Many rebels started burying their guns; some fled Mogadishu. There was confusion and tension everywhere. I couldn't wait to see *Mareekans* land in Mogadishu! Hopefully, they would look like actors in the movies and would completely overpower the militias.

And so at midnight on December 9, the thunderous roar of helicopters and gunships filled the air. Then came the buzz of hovercrafts, unloading tanks and marines onto the beach. The noises woke us up right away. Through the bullet holes in our roof, I could see the gleaming lights of the planes.

I couldn't wait to see the troops and the helicopters. At dawn Hassan and I, holding hands, walked down to the airport, passing streets that used to have sniper nests. As we got closer, the sounds of the helicopters became deafening. It seemed like everything was vibrating with noise and excitement. We joined a group of other eager Somalis looking at warships in the distance on the blue ocean; everywhere around the airport, marines in camouflage were taking positions and setting up gun posts. Someone said the *Mareekans* had rounded up the rebels who were controlling the airport and seaport.

The crowd got bigger and bigger; we shouted, laughed, and cheered in excitement. The *Mareekan* flag was waving over the airport, stars and stripes. That's when it hit me: I had seen that flag in movies! These *Mareekans* were definitely the movie people, and this was a real movie happening in front of us!

Commando must be here, I thought. *This is it.* This was the moment I had been waiting for, to meet Commando and watch him blow away all the militias!

I watched all day as the marines took positions, more and more of them coming. Humvees and tanks roamed noisily but never fired a shot. I was getting impatient for the battle to start. Hassan and I grew bolder and edged close to the troops. I stood there with my mouth open, watching them drink from water bottles and smile at us. I made a sign asking for water, and the white guy in uniform went into the Humvee and handed me a plastic bottle. Then we made eating signs with our hands to our mouths, and they handed us tasty marmalade, brcad, and butter.

One of the marines threw a chocolate candy to me. I grabbed it and swallowed the whole thing. When I got home and told Mom, she gave me a hard slap.

"You must not eat pork!" she said.

I told her I didn't think it was pork, it was swect, but she didn't believe me. How would she know what pork tasted like?

As evening fell, Mogadishu was noisier than I had ever heard it. But for the first time in two years, there was no sound of explosions and gunfire. Lights came from everywhere, helicopters, tents, cars. It looked like daytime in the middle of the night. But for the first time, my friends, my brother, and I could go out on the dusty streets after dark and play games, laugh, and talk. Falis's movie theater could now stay open at night, but we did not go. For the first time in years, outside was even more exciting than the movies.

One morning my brother and I woke to see Humvees parked in the streets of our neighborhood. The troops were going from house to house, searching for weapons. Unlike the militiamen, they looked fit and clean in their uniforms, which had no holes or missing buttons. They were not arguing with each other. I stood there trying to imagine the America that these people came from; that place must be gorgeous. Then a beautiful, tall female marine exited a house near us and walked our way. She had a huge smile on her face, but Hassan and I ran back to the house and stayed close to our mom and Khadija. We weren't sure what was happening, and we did not want our mom to be hurt. The lady came in and used sign language to communicate that she wanted to search the house for weapons. Every step she took, I was following her, my mom struggling to pull me away. Before she left, she smiled, said something, and came to me, stretching out her hand. I shook my head no and backed off shyly. I wanted to touch her, but I was too scared to get into trouble with my mom and Somali culture. Normally, we don't shake hands with women, especially a non-Muslim. The soldier wasn't angry, and she handed me some chocolate bars. My mom grabbed them away, thinking it was pork, but we convinced her it was candy. Even she ate some.

Food distribution centers opened in Mogadishu. Hassan and I went to one of the food kitchens in the old ministry building—the place we had crawled past every day to avoid snipers while bringing water. Now the snipers were gone and the gates were open, hundreds of people queuing for food. Hassan and I waited in line every day, holding bowls in our hands to get nutritional porridge for our family. People started flooding back into Mogadishu. The city of women and children now had men. One of them was our dad.

He wandered the streets confused, checking in the distribution centers, searching for anyone he knew. He looked at every family sleeping on the streets, hoping to see us and wondering if we were still alive. In the city where he once was a basketball star, no one recognized Tall Nur. The celebrity athlete was now homeless, hungry, and sick like everyone else. His feet were burning. He put on some discarded flip-flops he found along the road—two different sizes, but he didn't care, anything to shield his feet from the scorching ground. Dad was almost ready to collapse when he ran into Khadija's daughter Fatuma. She led him to our house, where Mom and Nima were taking their midday nap next to each other with bellies full of porridge.

When my mom saw her husband walk in after three years, she thought she was seeing a ghost. This man in front of her looked sort of like Nur Iftin, but different. He was so thin and dark, his eyes sunk deep in his head. He had rashes, cuts, and bruises all over his body. His hair had grown long and was matted with dust and mud. His shirt was torn.

Hassan and I were at the madrassa, memorizing our lesson for the day, when Khadija's daughter Fatuma came and told us. Macalin Basbaas, and the other kids who had believed Hassan and I were orphans like most of them, watched us sprint out of the school.

We had forgotten Dad's face during the past three years of the civil war, and like our mom, we felt we were reuniting with a ghost. I still remember the smell that was coming from Dad, of blood and dust. Hassan and I sat at his side. Our mom went out to fill a bucket with warm water for him to take a shower, but he was too weak, so she bathed him herself. Every time Mom touched his skin with the water, he screamed in pain. His long, muscly legs looked like sticks. Mom fed him with porridge that Hassan and I brought from the distribution center. Hassan cut his hair and trimmed his long beard. I washed his clothes; all he had was a *macawis* and the torn shirt. Mom put a straw mat in the corner of the house. He covered himself with a piece of cloth and slept deeply, waking only to pray five times a day. Finally, he was well enough to go to a clinic run by the United Nations for shots, penicillin tablets, and vitamins.

Back home, Dad finally told us all that had happened during his treacherous journey deep in the bush. After he left us in Baidoa, he walked for days into the bush, land he once crossed as a nomad with his camels. He met a group of Rahanweyn men sitting under an acacia tree. They had killed a gazelle and were sharing the meat over a fire. After discovering they all spoke the Maay dialect, they shared their meat with him. They were nomads who had never seen the city, so my dad's stories of his basketball games, the clubs, and the beach were all like fairy tales to them. They stayed together for months, constantly moving and hunting, sharing the meat according to nomad tradition. At times they hummed, sang, and danced, and at night they slept, with only one man awake to guard their camp. Like my dad, they had all lost contact with their families, but they did their best to enjoy the few months they spent together as nomads again.

One day they heard gunshots and had to scatter and run for their lives again. Dad eventually caught up with one of the men. They walked for days, unsure where they were going. At times they came across corpses that were rotting and marred. Dad thought for sure that we were dead by now. Even if we had escaped the militias, the harsh environment would most certainly kill us.

The night the U.S. Marines landed in Mogadishu, Dad was looking up at the stars, still hiding in the bush, not knowing what was happening in the city. A few months later he was able to return to Baidoa after he heard that Australian and American troops were there, providing food and nutrition.

Dad stayed in Baidoa after reuniting with a friend there. He'd walk into the bush around Baidoa, trying to see if he could find us. Finally, he gave up and assumed we were dead. But then, after hearing that lots of people had returned from Baidoa to Mogadishu, he decided to go back to the city and look for us.

After Dad told his story, we told him ours. He was not surprised that our mom had done everything to save us. He was sitting with his back against the tree trunk, sleepily, but he leaned forward and looked at Hassan and me, telling us how proud we made him for the way we had helped our mom and sisters.

It would take a long time for his health to return. Sometimes he talked to Mom about life in the good times before the wars—their life in the bush and in Mogadishu. Sometimes he paced back and forth in the house, reading the Koran. It was Hassan and I who had taken the full responsibility of feeding our family every day, including our weakened dad, the once-famous national athlete.

■ ■ ■

The year had changed to 1993, my ninth year of life. Troops from the U.S. and the United Nations had been in the city for a month. We would see them jogging, and swimming in the green waters off the beach. One woman, some type of aid worker, jogged every morning near our house. She was white, had long hair, and smiled and remembered my name. I made sure to get up every morning and say hi to her when she passed. I watched her listening to music on her headphones and stretching. Sometimes she would sit and play games with me, my brother, and Nima. She always brought us snacks like peanuts, candies, and cookies, and she also brought painkillers, antibiotics, and other medicine. She explained what they were for and how to take them. I think I fell in love with this woman. It wasn't romantic; I just wanted to stay close to her. Then one day we stopped seeing her. Soon we realized no one was jogging anymore.

The warlords were getting restless; they wanted the city

back. Aidid had a radio station and was telling Somalis on the air that they should fight the "occupation" of Mogadishu. On June 5, UN forces went to the radio station to seize weapons. Aidid thought they were trying to shut down the broadcasts, and he ambushed the troops, killing twenty-four Pakistani soldiers. That's when things got really bad.

On July 12, the Americans sent Cobra helicopters over a house in Mogadishu where they thought Aidid was hiding and blasted it into rubble. He wasn't there—but dozens of other people were killed. Aidid claimed the Americans had killed women and children, and he started to whip up Somalis against the infidel "invaders." The Americans said only Aidid's soldiers had been in the house, but the seed of resentment against the foreigners had been sown. Aidid wasted no time, planting roadside bombs in August that killed four American soldiers and wounded seven others. The Battle of Mogadishu had begun.

I had been waiting so long for this moment! I wanted to see the American troops in action and how they fight. Soon, Cobras and Black Hawks were swooping down everywhere, hovering over buildings where militiamen were hiding. I looked up and cheered whenever the helicopters shot at a building; to me it seemed like the greatest movie.

I thought the airplanes and helicopters would scare the militias away, but instead the huge, strong American men of the movies were being chased by Somali rebels on the streets. It was not what I expected. Soon everything had changed. We were no longer welcome near the marines;

there were no more candies or cookies. For the first time the marines were aiming their guns at Somalis and pushing them around, even us kids. They looked nervous.

It is hard to explain why so many Mogadishans turned against the marines and cheered the militias. The rebels had been killing us for four years, stealing our food, and defecating in our houses. The Americans had been generous. The U.S. attack on the house that killed so many civilians was surely part of the cause. And at this point, we were so familiar with death and destruction that this new battle seemed like a basketball game; it was not like real life. People filled the streets, rooting for their home team. I too fell in with the crowd. I yelled out to the militias to let them know which side the helicopter was coming from. I threw rocks at helicopters. I ran with the crowd, repeating their cheers: "Up with Aidid! Down with America!"

The battle continued for weeks. Every night from our house I watched militiamen changing positions, shooting at helicopters. For a few minutes it would be dead quiet, then the helicopter would swoop down again and fire back. With all this violence overhead, not just in the streets, we prayed for safety.

On October 3, Aidid's forces shot down two Black Hawk helicopters with rocket-propelled grenades. I heard the booming explosions about a mile from our house. Naturally, I ran as fast as I could to watch this new action unfold. Everything was so dusty I could not see much or get very close. A crowd was dragging the bodies of dead Americans, and people said others were still alive, trapped. The rescue operation lasted until the next day. More than three hundred Somalis died, and sixteen Americans. A few days later, I was playing hide-and-seek in the remains of one of the Black Hawks.

■ ■ ■

Five months later, the Americans left Mogadishu. It was March 1994, my tenth year. The skinny rebels with their ugly brown teeth had beaten off the movie-star marines. The Americans and the UN troops left so fast they didn't even take their stuff. They left behind malfunctioning helicopters and vehicles, boots and uniforms. I joined a crowd that went to the same spot where the *Mareekans* had first invited us to watch them land on the beach in hovercrafts. This time we were taking the stuff they left behind, even the boxes of medicines, tablets, discarded syringes.

The same militias whom we had cheered for against the foreigners would soon turn on us again—stealing our food and shooting at us for sport. I felt shame that I had cheered against the Americans, the people who came to help us from the country of my dreams. But I now realize that I was lost—a little boy caught among the teachings of Macalin Basbaas, my mom and her view on infidels, the American troops and their kindness and food, my love for my brave dad and the glorious Somali basketball team, and the American movies I adored.

I stood on the beach, picking through the discarded

camouflage uniforms with the American names sewn above the pockets. I held them up, hoping one would fit my skinny little body. My friends Mohammed, Bashi, and Bocow laughed. I looked at them and scowled.

"I'm not Somali," I said. "I am *Mareekan*. I was left behind by the marines. And they will come for me soon."

THE ONE THEY CALL AMERICAN

The city of women and children had become a city of refugees. The streets swarmed with former herders and farmers, most of them Maay-speaking Rahanweyn from where my parents came. They had initially come to Mogadishu for the food brought by the UN forces and to seek work. In the meantime, their ancestral lands, the bush, had been overrun by the warlords. Now they could not go home.

The Hawiye of Mogadishu did not know much about the refugees and assumed they were mostly criminals. Some of the very poorest Rahanweyn were in a subclan known as the Eelaay. They wore amulets and often lived by begging instead of herding animals. Because of these Eelaay people, the Hawiye assumed that all Rahanweyn were beggars. To many Mogadishans they were all disgusting. But my mom would often go outside to help these Rahanweyn refugees find places to sleep.

Some of the Rahanweyn beggars would come to Khadija's house early in the morning around five to beg for a cup of tea. Mom was usually up then, making tea for my dad, and when the beggars came and spoke in their Maay dialect, she would respond in Maay, *"See hayteng?"*—How are you? *"Hadhawaw fadheew."*—Come in, have a seat. Mom and the beggars would get into deep conversations as they sipped tea in the house. They talked about how bad life had turned under the Hawiye militias. They talked about the animals, the nomad life. Many of these beggars in Mogadishu had once been some of the wealthiest people in their villages; they had owned hundreds of camels, cows, and goats— assets they thought would never disappear. But like my parents, they had not even a chicken today, nor a place to live. They bragged about their past life. They talked about fighting hyenas, lions, and cheetahs. They were warriors who fought with knives, spears, and bows. They had no idea why God had abandoned them and left them begging on the streets.

Hassan and I identified with these beggars. We would have been like them had we not been born in Mogadishu and been taken in by our neighbor Khadija. Still, no one else we knew let beggars into their houses, and Hassan and I were a little embarrassed by Mom inviting them inside. By now we had started to distance ourselves from our parents. We had no stories of our own to tell about the villages, or the nomad life. All we knew was Mogadishu. We had a

Mogadishu accent, the neighborhood was our home, and all our friends were Mogadishan. We had become so unlike our parents, who pined for their village. Hassan and I hoped they would not move us all to a village in the bush.

Then one day, none of the beggars showed up. Mom went out to see what had happened. Down the street, around a corner, her beggar friends had all been killed by a Hawiye sniper. This kind of horrifying violence was very common in Mogadishu, but that didn't make it any less tragic to Mom. Quietly, she returned home and prayed for them to enter heaven.

The Hawiye clan's harassment of the Rahanweyn continued and grew worse. Already weak and confined to the house, Dad was despairing. He was worried that if he ever did get up the strength to walk around, he would be attacked by Hawiye gangs. So he retreated further into his small world and his bored mind.

He never left Khadija's compound. Her family could give us only one room, and Hassan, Mom, Nima, and I crammed into it. There was no space for Dad; he had to spend the night outside exposed to mosquitoes. So we took shifts: he slept during the day in our room when we all went out; by night he sat outside in the courtyard, swatting mosquitoes and praying. Gone was the strong man who jumped over fences, chased lions, and scored hoops. Whenever he stood, he leaned on a stick, his tall body bent in half. The brave dad who carried us on his shoulders now needed help with everything—getting to the bathroom, showering, dressing. Hassan and I sometimes snuck out to escape the work. I would go to the movies, and Hassan would disappear with his friends. We would be out all day and come back with so much to do for Dad. We had to wash his clothes, trim his hair, and walk him around the house.

My dad could not understand why all this had happened to him and his family. When he had money and played for the national team, he had always given to charity, given money to the poor, helped everyone. Why did he deserve this misery? Had his prayers not worked? Now he could not go to the mosque, but he had a prayer mat in the house. The prayers kept him alive, but he had so much guilt. "I used to go to movies, went to clubs, and traveled abroad," he told me once. "God might be angry with all that sin." He believed those sinful things could explain why he suffered and lost his wealth.

Is he also sending me a message not to go to the movies? I wondered.

Every day, I walked out to the airport, hoping to see the American marines coming back to rescue me. The airport had been closed since the troops pulled out, and quickly the militias took over the terminals. There was no commander they listened to, no schedules to follow. They intimidated innocent people with guns and growling engines. Their technicals, loaded with qat leaves, barreled into Mogadishu with engines screaming, like teenage drag racers trying to impress each other. This juvenile display of power reminded us every day that these were the rabble that had kicked American marines out of the city.

Other than sheikhs, the only role models for young men

in Mogadishu were these rebel soldiers with their guns, their endless bickering and cursing. They influenced us. I cursed every day at my friends for fun, and they cursed back. Our fiercest obscenities were related to pigs and dogs, two animals much hated in Mogadishu. "Son of a dog!" "Son of a pig!" "Your dad is a dog and you are a dog!" Everyone would get very angry when associated with these dirty, evil animals that cannot be touched. When I saw Americans kissing dogs in movies, I'd make a face. "How do they trust the dog?" I asked myself. "What if the dog bites them?"

One day Dad called us out to the courtyard. "I'm going to take a walk around to see if my brother Hassan is still in his house," he said. Dad had not left the house since the Americans and United Nations left, so this was a big step. In Mogadishu under the warlords, it was very dangerous to knock on people's doors, especially for a Rahanweyn. None of us had been to our uncle's house since we returned to Mogadishu, and we didn't know who was living there.

But Dad found the courage to walk to the house. Leaning on his stick, in his worn-out clothes, he looked like one of the Rahanweyn beggars. People avoided him on the street. He remained unfazed, looking around. Everything had changed, no more clubs and restaurants, no cheering fans slapping his back.

Uncle Hassan's house was there, still standing, but very damaged. The green tin door that my dad remembered was not there; instead, a gate of thorn branches covered the entrance. He stood there hesitating, deciding whether to move the thorn gate and go inside; many houses had been looted and taken over by militiamen and their families. Who lived here now?

It turns out, he didn't have to worry. Dhuha, Hassan's wife, and her daughters greeted Dad, welcoming him inside. Everyone cried; they hugged. They told Dad how Hassan had been killed by a bullet. Dad had no more tears to cry. His own parents had starved to death or were eaten by animals, who knows? His other siblings had gone missing and were presumed dead. Dad reminded the grieving family that his brother Hassan was by now in heaven and that we will all die and go where the dead are.

"We are happy you are here for us," said Dhuha.

But Dad was in no position to support their family; he couldn't even support his own family. Even if it were possible for my dad to care for Hassan's family, with the wars still happening, and men being killed daily, he might be next. He reminded Dhuha about this, saying he did not want to cause more grief to her family. My aunt Dhuha said she understood, then invited us to come and move into the two-room mud house that had been built on Uncle Hassan's property. This was a relief to us, because now Hassan and I would have our own room. Dad, Mom, and Nima would stay in the other room. Nima had turned seven, but she looked somehow both younger and older—small and frail from years of malnutrition—and was still struggling to speak well.

Now we woke up every morning alongside family members, which made Dad feel better. He and Dhuha would sit and talk while Mom and Dhuha's kids were busy doing the chores. (Dhuha was older than my mom and also had two grown daughters, so she was excused from housework.) Sometimes we shared sweet tea with cloves, cinnamon, and camel milk. Only one full kettle was made at a time; everything was measured, from tea to water. We were told we could shower only once a week with a three-liter jerry can, and we were given just five minutes each to use the bathroom. The most difficult rule was the curfew: everyone had to be at home no later than seven in the evening. Mogadishu was completely lawless, and crime in the city was high at night; there were burglars and people with guns and knives.

Our new room was so much better than Khadija's tin-and-cardboard shack. The room for Hassan and me had only one straw mat, no furniture, no beds. But it had a wood-framed window, and we could sneak out through that window and come back in without anyone noticing us. We had to be so quiet because the wall between our room and our parents' room had cracks and holes from bullets and rockets, and we could be heard when we came in or when we talked. Whenever we lay on our mat talking, Mom would yell at us to go to sleep.

At night, our room was pitch-black. We had no electricity or lantern, but we could see the glittering stars through the small window. As we both lay on the mat on the dirt floor, Hassan talked about Kenya, Yemen, Europe, and America. "Arnold Schwarzenegger and Sylvester Stallone visit Kenya on their vacations," he said, a fib that nonetheless caught my attention. "Nairobi is like New York," he continued. "They have highways, nightlife, clubs, music, movie theaters. And a lot of white people."

I imagined either city was no closer than the stars we saw through the holes in our roof.

"I want to leave Somalia," said Hassan.

"You are dreaming," I said. To me, leaving Somalia seemed impossible. And how could I live without Hassan? Besides, at that point I was not unhappy with my life. Life in Somalia was harsh, but it was all I knew. You wake up in the morning with no plans and no future. Every day is the same. They come and go; months come and go. No New Year's celebrations, no holidays, no birthday parties. Even the Eid was nothing to look forward to in war-torn Mogadishu. The Eid is the biggest Muslim celebration, coming after the last day of Ramadan, like Christmas in the West. In good times, kids get to dress in brand-new clothes and buy toys and sweets. But since 1991, the Eid in Somalia was just like every other day. No clothes, no toys, no sweets. All we had was our mom telling us stories about the fun Eid holidays we'd had before the war.

While many people like my brother dreamed of moving abroad, I found peace sitting at Falis's video shack, watching movies. The things I saw in the movies seemed unreachable, but at least I could learn the language they spoke. I had been making progress on picking up words. I would sit very close to the speaker and pay close attention to what the American actors were saying. Sometimes even when the dialogue was in English, the movie had English subtitles, which made it easier to learn how to write the words. I also learned about the culture. The movies often showed kids' rooms decorated with posters of rock and movie stars, which inspired me to decorate my own room. I collected old, worn-out posters I had found in the ruins of the Cinema Ecuatore and other buildings—posters of Michael Jackson, Madonna, Sylvester Stallone, Arnold Schwarzenegger, Bruce Willis. I would use the sap from the apple of the Sodom plant to glue the posters onto the walls of our room. Using a piece of charcoal from the madrassa, I wrote on the walls the English words I had learned from movies, plus movie titles, names of stars I liked, and some daily phrases I taught myself, most of them swear words. I liked it when actors in the movies swore.

I also wrote a notice on our wooden door: "Stop. No coming." I meant for people not to come into our room, but of course no one would ever be able to read that. When Mom saw the walls tattooed in English, she gasped.

Dad was furious. "I never expected this!" he said, pointing at the poster of Madonna. "What is this? Is this why we sent you to the madrassa? Are you out of your mind?" They both kept yelling at us for being evil and littering our home with infidels. Finally, Mom tore off all the posters and erased all the words as best she could. I was forced to scrub the walls with water. When she told Macalin Basbaas, I was whipped. From this time on, whenever something bad happened, I was blamed for bringing evil to the house. One time a stray bullet hit the roof, my fault. Another time, Nima was coughing and wheezing and I was blamed for it. The posters and the things I wrote just became a huge problem for me in our house.

Even while I was scrubbing English off my bedroom walls, I was writing new words on the walls of abandoned houses where no one could scold me. I wrote, "I am not lost," which I learned from the movie *Die Hard*. Then I painted the American flag, a huge one, on the wall with the stars and stripes. My friends looked at the words and wondered what they meant, so I translated for them.

Learning Arabic or reading the Koran was the only thing my parents wanted me to do. But I had my brother at my back, himself inspired by movies. We found joy in talking about movies, English, actors, singers. We practiced English more than we practiced Arabic. We didn't have enough vocabulary to say much, our grammar was not perfect, but we got better. We collected English words from old worn-out magazines found on the streets. I used them as textbooks, underlining phrases and words I thought were good. I noticed they used many prepositions, such as "over," "down," and "up," and we were confused about when to use them. So Hassan and I practiced, building our own sentences. "*Down* here, *over* your head, get *over* to Mom."

Every night after Dad listened to the BBC Somali Service, Hassan and I would tune in to the six o'clock English-learning program by the Voice of America, called *New Dynamic English*. The show featured two characters, Max and Kathy, who talked about American culture, U.S. cities, and how to speak American English. The shortwave broadcast had a lot of static, and the lessons were hard to understand sometimes, but we listened carefully anyway. When Mom or Dad found out, they would snatch the radio from us and tell us, "Go say the evening prayers. Go to the mosque."

We went to the movies instead. Hassan and I held hands walking in the dark to the movies and back. We would get home after nine; by then our dad was the only person awake, reciting his regular prayers, or sitting in a corner of the house in the dark with his head leaning against his hand, looking up in despair and boredom. Mom and Nima were deep asleep after a long day laboring—washing, cooking, cleaning. We would tiptoe into our room from the window and quietly spread our sleeping mat.

Friday was the weekend in Somalia, the only day off from the madrassa. My friends and I gathered under the shade of neem trees. Often we played games until noon, when the mosques of Mogadishu all rang the call for the important Friday prayers, called *Qudbah*. Huge crowds of mosquegoers filled up the streets, except the militiamen, who sat in the beds of their technicals, ignoring the call to prayer. The rest of us had to sit through an hour-long lecture by the imam before we stood up for the prayers. In the lecture, the imam talked about how sinful it was to watch movies, how non-Muslim nations were planning to eliminate Islam by trying to spread their languages, including English, their culture through movies and songs, and soccer. Hundreds of men in the mosque all nodded along, my brother and I as well.

Macalin Basbaas was always seated in the front row very close to the imam. He never missed one Friday. One day he took the microphone and mentioned many names of his students who go to movies, and he asked for everyone to pray that the sinful students would return to the Islamic culture and stop watching movies. My name, of course, was among the ones mentioned. When the prayer ended and men started pouring out of the mosque, an imam took the mic and asked for those whose names had been mentioned to stay behind. I sat on the floor with the other sinful, nervous boys who were called. Six men, with beards almost touching their chests and with fierce eyes, surrounded us and scolded us.

I felt pressure from all sides—the imam, Macalin Basbaas, my parents—but still I kept going to the movies. We also played soccer. We could not afford a real soccer ball, so we made our own from old clothes, rubbish, and shredded plastic, all tied together to look like a ball. Our goalposts were made of sticks. We had no cleats of course; we played barefoot, tackling each other and scoring wild goals to the cheers of our teammates and the boos of our opponents. Before heading home, I'd dust myself off so my parents would never guess I'd been playing sports. When Mom asked where I was, I always told her I was at the mosque reading the Koran.

Nights were always a good time for my English practice at the movies. My friends would come find me at Falis's, now appreciating my basic English skills. They sat close to me because it was my job to tell them what the actors were saying. My translating became more accurate; people knew this because events in the movie happened the way I predicted, based on the dialogue. "They are planning to kidnap the little girl!" I would shout. And the girl gets kidnapped. I became known at the movie shack as the translator. Little did I know that someday that would become my full-time job.

Outside the movie shack, life went on at the madrassa. Children graduate as soon as they have memorized the entire Koran. That motivated me to study hard. I wanted to get out of there. We had to completely memorize over six thousand verses, and we had to know which verse is next to which without looking at the book. I was surprised to find myself able to memorize easily, just like I was memorizing English, and do the recitation with Macalin Basbaas. My parents were so proud of this, and they waited eagerly for the day I completed madrassa. They had plans for me. They wanted me to follow in the footsteps of Macalin Basbaas and all the other pious men in the city who carried Korans, not guns, and gathered around mosques every day.

But I had other plans. Falis had started letting me into the movies free of charge—without having to sweep the floor—because I could attract a crowd who were enthusiastic to hear my translations. They encouraged me to learn more and listen. It was fun to have a crowd all leaning their heads toward me, listening. Unlike at the mosque or the madrassa, in the video shack we could talk, shout, laugh. But as soon as the movie ended, we ran home because we had to be up at six in the morning to go to madrassa.

Learning English and American culture started as something for fun, an escape from the miseries of our life. But soon it became more than entertainment. I was discovering the world beyond Somalia and learning that I could make my own decisions about my life. I learned from movies that no one should be above the law. That people could be held responsible for their actions. I learned the freedom of women doing things men can do. In some movies, I could see kids going to school in buses the color of Falis's turmeric makeup; I wanted to go to a real school in a yellow bus and learn things besides the Koran. I learned that not all Americans are white; there are black people there who stand shoulder to shoulder with the whites. I wondered when Somalia would catch up to some of the ways of life I saw in the movies.

When I asked my parents why Somalia was behind and in a total mess, they always replied that it was Allah's will. He put us in this mess; he is the only one who can get us out of this. How can you argue with that? But somewhere in my head I told myself, *Allah is not responsible for this mess; why would he do that?* Somali militias were the ones who bombed our house, killed my uncle, and shot at us while we went to fetch water. It was not Allah.

The learning continued for me. I learned that all white people are not the same; they don't speak the same language, they don't use the same money, they don't live in one country, they don't even have the same religion. Some even don't eat pork.

"Mom, there are some white people who don't eat pork," I said one day.

"Shut up!" she said.

"And, Mom, America is not next to Somalia."

"I said shut up!"

One night as we lay on our backs on a mat looking up at the stars, I told Mom, "The moving stars are not lucky stars; some of them are satellites."

"What is a *satellite*?" she asked.

"They are moving machines or ships crossing the skies."

"You are being misinformed, Abdi, shut up!"

"Mom, there are nine planets among the stars too."

"The Koran tells us there are seven," she said. "Shut up and don't try to say anything about that." I went quiet and kept listening to Mom's stories of how the blinking stars are our ancestors trying to communicate. This time, I did not believe her.

I don't blame my parents; they had been trying to make me be a good person, even though being good can take many forms. Whenever I started arguing with my mom about things like satellites, she blamed the movies. "Those evil movies that you go to are making you very stupid!" she would say. "You have let the devil take over you!" She was especially mad that the movies were distracting me from becoming her dream son, a sheikh.

Even though my mom despised my movie habit, I earned a new privilege: because I was near graduating from the madrassa, I was now allowed to bring my friends to our house.

In my room we talked endlessly about stories in the movies. They listened as I spoke English and tried to teach them. "'How are you, how are you doing, how is it going?' . . . these are all the same," I told them. "They all mean the same."

Sometimes we went to the Sufi mosque, where they didn't even care if we spoke English. The Sufis were not so strict; they just minded their chants and ceremonies without telling people what to do. Macalin Basbaas never went to that mosque; he cursed the Sufis as evil, but Hassan and I liked to listen to the chanting. It was so peaceful and mysterious. I fell in love with those gentle people. Later the radical Islamists destroyed their tombs and erased their culture from most of southern Somalia.

● ● ●

By 1996, the video shack was no longer the only entertainment in Mogadishu. The warlords still fought and shot their guns constantly, but some culture and normal life were returning to Mogadishu. One big change was public transportation. Some men who returned to the city had converted Toyota pickup trucks into buses by putting seats in the back, charging a few coins for rides. These buses, called *xaajiyo khamsiin*, meant we could explore parts of the city outside our neighborhood. The bus drivers risked their lives every single day, negotiating with dangerous militias who would block the roads.

I'd go to the famous street of Via Roma, with its fine buildings with arches, terraces, and shady trees. Tall coconut palms swayed in the breeze. So much had been destroyed by militias, but stores reopened in renovated buildings. I walked up the road toward the beach. Owners were standing at their shop doors, calling out to passersby. On the walls, they had painted pictures of popular snacks like *bur* (sweet doughnut holes), *bajiyas* (savory doughnuts made from crushed and skinned black-eyed peas with onion, garlic, and tomatoes), and especially samosas, the fried meat-filled pastries.

I loved to go to a candy store on Via Roma called Xalwo Shakata. One day, after stuffing my face with sweets, I heard strange music blasting out of the entrance of the building next door. A small wooden sign, written in chalk, read, "Al-Faghi Studio and Stereo." On the wall were photos of Michael Jackson and Stevie Wonder, and someone had written their names in Anglicized Somali: "Maaykal Jaksan," "Stiif Wandhar." The wooden door shook with loud music; a crowd of people were practicing wild dance moves in front of the building. Some people walking by covered their ears with their hands. The music was not Motown or soul, which I had heard before—it was something new. I stood there in awe. I tried to enter, but the DJ wouldn't let kids inside. Still, I could hear the music outside and twist my body like other people on the sidewalk. A crowd had built up, everyone dancing and laughing, and someone told me the music was American and called hip-hop and rap, and also some music from Jamaica called reggae.

This was the beginning of my new life. Al-Faghi became

my favorite place to go every day, practicing how to dance with the crowd on the sidewalk. When I got home, I practiced by myself. Tupac Shakur and Bob Marley became my favorite artists after Michael Jackson. I decided if I was going to talk like an American, I should also dance like one. I got myself a cheap boom box and some tapes. Soon, I felt ready to show my dance skills in my neighborhood. Mom would find me on the streets dancing with the boom box and scowl. "Stupid boy!" she said. I had to sneak the boom box into our room through the window and hide it by digging the dirt and burying it under the mat so that when Mom came in, she would not see it.

The hip-hop culture was spreading fast into Mogadishu. All the young people who weren't trying to become sheikhs started wearing hip-hop fashion that we saw on television and posters. The people who ran Al-Faghi were young men who had just returned from Yemen and came with some cash to establish a music store. Similarly, the Bakara market was booming with small clothing businesses. The clothes were brought in from Kenya, Yemen, and Ethiopia. For just a few shillings, I was able to buy a black baseball cap that said "Titanic" and baggy denim jeans. I found a few plastic bracelets to wear on my wrists and a bandanna for a do-rag head scarf. With my cap twisted sideways and my pants sagging below my waist, I practiced walking with a swagger; my friends Bashi and Bocow did the same thing, and we called ourselves a posse. This was all good timing, because I was starting to get interested in girls, and by now in Mogadishu, girls were falling only for boys who could dance and who dressed in jeans.

The new hip-hop culture disgusted the Somali elders, who started calling us *saqajaan*, "idiots"—but we weren't trying to impress them. My dance skills and ability to speak English made me popular with all the young people in the neighborhood. Soon people were coming to my house, asking my mom, "Is Abdi American here?" She was so mad when she learned I was the one they call American. To her, American meant Christian, and a betrayal of my Muslim heritage. My friends Bocow, Bashi, and Mohammed now regretted not paying as much attention when we all sat at the shack watching movies. They were still just regular Somalis on the street, while I was becoming the neighborhood star.

Around this time, Hassan and I started to drift apart. For one thing, he couldn't play soccer because of a childhood injury. From that day he always walked with a slight limp. Nor did he go to movies as much as I did. But he had his own friends, Mohamed, Daud, and Hussein, and they got interested in raising pigeons. Hassan took care of the birds, and he and his friends would race them—carrying them away from the house, letting them go, and seeing which would fly home first. Our male pigeon Gariirka was always so fast and clever and surprised everyone, winning over and over again.

Hassan should have been ahead of me at the madrassa, but he lost interest in memorizing verses. Finally the pressure became too much for him; he defied our parents and Macalin Basbaas and dropped out of school a little before graduating. When a student drops out, his parents disown him. My mom told Hassan not to come back to the house again. Just like that, my brother was living on the streets.

· 7 ·

BUUFIS

One late April morning in the year 2000, I woke with a smiling face and walked to the madrassa at six. There I wrote down the last lesson on my board—the end of Surat al-Baqarah, the final Koranic chapter. I was so excited! This meant I could graduate from school and go anywhere in the city, dance, and watch movies, without worrying about Macalin Basbaas and his beatings. I had memorized all 114 chapters of the Koran—fluently reading 6,266 verses in perfect Arabic. The day I came home from my last lesson, Mom had a huge smile on her face. As a gift, she had bought me a white kanzu, the robe worn by sheikhs, and a *tisbih*, the necklace of Islamic prayer beads.

A few days later we gathered for a brief party at the madrassa, ten of us who graduated that day, looking forward to a world without school. Macalin Basbaas made a very long speech, still holding his bunch of sticks tied together in his hands, ready to administer some last-minute pain.

"This is the moment that your parents have been waiting for," he said.

Not as much as we have, I thought.

"This is the beginning of your future," he continued. "You all need to go out and spread the word." That meant Macalin Basbaas wanted us to open madrassas of our own or be at the mosque permanently every day. And for some graduates, this was a dream. They dreamed of going to Saudi Arabia or Egypt to pursue Islamic studies. But I had other dreams on my mind.

I felt very accomplished; I had survived seven years of beatings from Macalin Basbaas. Was it possible to learn the Koran without being beaten? I felt certain I would not have succeeded without the threat of those sticks. But when I saw and felt the scars across my body, I knew I could never beat children like that. I could never be a madrassa teacher.

To celebrate graduation, we went to Falis's video shack with no worries about waking up at six the next morning or reciting the lesson for the day. The movie was a new one for us, called *Coming to America*, starring Eddie Murphy as an African prince who goes to America to find a bride. I translated as usual.

Little did I know, while I was at the movie celebrating graduation, my mom had been chatting with Aunt Dhuha and some other women in the neighborhood. As usual, Dhuha bragged about her three sons, who had become sheikhs. They dressed in robes, went to the mosque all day, and read the Koran. Other women talked about their sons opening new madrassas and teaching the Koran to young Mogadishans. It had given Mom ideas.

I got home in the evening to see Mom and Dhuha sitting happily. Dad had slaughtered a chicken; he was pulling the feathers out. It was a graduation gift for me. I sat down, happily drinking a glass of cold camel milk, hungering for chicken meat. I went into my room and saw a fresh cloth spread on my mat, a gift from Dhuha. Then Mom walked into my room with Dhuha.

"Abdi," she said, "tomorrow you need to go back to the madrassa and start as the assistant to Macalin Basbaas."

I felt like someone had fired a gun at me.

"We arranged it all with Macalin Basbaas," she continued. "He will be waiting for you tomorrow."

"But I need a break from the madrassa!" I protested.

"A break?" she yelled. "You don't need a break at all; you need to go to Macalin Basbaas tomorrow! You are not a student anymore, but you can have your own madrassa someday, and to do that, you need to stick with him. He will show you the way to be a sheikh."

"Mom, I don't want to!" I stormed out of the house.

Mom kept pressuring me to go back to the madrassa and practice more. She also insisted that I go to the mosque regularly. I withheld my anger, but the final straw came a few weeks after my graduation, when the Tabliiq knocked on our door. The Tabliiq are proselytizers in the Muslim world—Sunni men who go around the city encouraging people to go to the mosque daily. When they came to our house to take me, I refused. My mom thought I was a lost cause. Gone forever was her dream of my being a respected sheikh with a shaved head, who hates music and reads the Koran all day. My parents kicked me out of the house. I was fourteen years old, and I went looking for my brother.

By day, Hassan hung around Zobe Square, which was crowded with elders and militiamen who gathered to talk about politics and clan rivalries. They cursed at each other and then cursed America and Israel for the invasion of Palestine. Hassan idled around nervously, always looking over his shoulder to avoid militia recruiters. He was fifteen and so tall for his age. Now that he was old enough to carry a gun, his choices grew even narrower. And once the recruiters started pressuring a person into joining their ranks, it was almost impossible to escape. Now I was out on the streets with him, dodging the militias and ducking when we heard gunfire.

By now, the northern Madinah district, where the hospital was located, had been taken over by a crime gang called Ciyaal Faacali. These young men had emerged from the ashes of the civil war, with no police or laws to stop them. They not only robbed people but also committed brutalities not seen in the southern parts of the city.

Hassan and I were careful to avoid such high-crime areas and street gangs. Throughout Mogadishu, people were crowding into the safer southern part of town, where our parents lived, and the neighborhood became dense with families and shops. Two movie theaters opened, the

Cinema Mogadishu and Cinema Ducale. Stereo stores popped up in other neighborhoods, selling cassette tapes and sound systems and even making recordings. My friends and I went to one of these stores to record our own rap songs on a tape. We rapped in a mix of Somali and English, describing a girl with hair like an ostrich and a walk like a camel. We sang English chorus lines like "She's the best!" "Come to me, babe!" "Dance with me, babe!" I felt like I was part of this new musical revolution and we were creating something amazing.

My parents were still mad at me, so I never went home. I slept on the streets at night, covering my head with the shirt I was wearing. By dawn the early-morning prayers broadcast from speakers on the minarets of the mosque woke me up. My friends Bocow and Bashi had also been kicked out of their families' houses, and they stayed with me on the streets.

Even though many people had returned to Mogadishu, there were still empty houses, most of them crawling with giant bugs, littered with trash and feces, and stiflingly hot. We hung around in those houses sometimes to eat and talk, but it was much better to sleep outside in the fresh air. I would sneak around to the back of our house when I was hungry, peeking through the holes to make sure Macalin Basbaas wasn't over, visiting Mom. When she was taking a nap and Dad was listening to the BBC Somali Service, I would quietly jump in the window. I scooped maize into my pockets and jumped out to the street, to share with my friends. They did the same for me. We walked to the beach to wash our clothes in the ocean.

I still prayed, and I respected the Muslim teachings about charity and justice. I consider myself a good Muslim to this day. But I had seen from the movies what was out in the world, and I didn't want the life my parents wanted for me. I wasn't going to spend all my life in a mosque.

● ● ●

Starting in 1998, Somalia had some good rainy seasons that soaked Mogadishu. I remember my mom saying it rained because the warlord Aidid had been killed just a year before, during a shoot-out among his own clan. With the rain, new life quickly emerged. There were butterflies and dragonflies floating around everywhere, and small lizards. The rain also brought back the flowers and their sweet fragrance, scents I have not found anywhere else in the world since.

But the rains also came with mosquitoes that carried malaria. It was getting hard for me to sleep outside with the sound of mosquitoes in my ears, followed by their painful bites. I decided to go back home. My mom saw the scratches on my body, the bites, sores, and bruises all over my face and hands. My brother, Hassan, also came home briefly, devoured by the insects and looking sick with malaria. Together, he and I slept in our old room, the rain hitting the roof overhead. During huge downpours, we ran out in the courtyard, filling any container we could find, even cups and bowls, to collect drinking water.

Everyone seemed to be forgetting about the war. No-mads like my mom were happy because, to them, rain was a sign of prosperity. She started humming the nomad songs for her goats and called out to her flock, even though they were gone forever. She ran around in the rain, laughing. I couldn't remember the last time I had seen my mom happy like that.

With no more Koran lessons, I could spend even more time learning English. I recorded the sound from the mov-ies on a cassette player, then replayed it constantly, listen-ing to the words. I practiced English freely on the streets, talking either to myself or to my brother or to my friends. I told people that in America you feel free, you can be a singer or an actor, anything you want.

I started teaching English to a group of boys and girls in the neighborhood when I was about fifteen. I put together the lessons myself, trying to think of easy ways the chil-dren could learn and charging a few coins. No one thought I could pull these lessons off, but soon my three students turned into ten. The lessons were repeated every week until each student memorized the passages—just like I had learned the Koran. My madrassa training had not gone to waste. Unlike Macalin Basbaas, I did not beat my students; in fact, I encouraged them to have fun. I would ask two stu-dents to stand up and face each other and practice the les-son by having a conversation. During the lessons, I would wear my blue jeans, my new long T-shirt, and sneakers. As I taught class, I would swagger and move around like a rapper. The students seemed to think I was very cool, this Somali guy who spoke English and danced like Snoop Dogg. I thought I was pretty cool too.

•••

By the year 2000, Mogadishu was divided into two economic classes: those who had relatives abroad, and those who didn't. Our family was in the second group. The others received money from family in faraway places Hassan and I dreamed of seeing, called Minnesota, Seattle, London, Toronto.

Somalis who had made it to those places were lucky to escape the country. Eventually, they had been resettled in North America and Europe from refugee camps in Kenya and Yemen. They found jobs in the West cleaning hotels, stacking shelves at Walmart, and driving taxicabs. And they saved up to send hundreds of dollars back to their relatives in Mogadishu. We thought they must be getting so rich.

I had no one in America, not even a distant relative. I felt it was unfair for me not to be able to collect dollars.

People who got money from America and Europe ate freshly cooked beans, rice, meat, and eggs. At our house we were struggling just to get corn. Our mom went out every day to work, walking miles into Bakara market to get a porter job for people who bought sacks of rice with dollars received from abroad. Mom would put the whole sack on her back, trudging miles to the rich person's house. With the cash she made, she would buy food for us.

Dad had gained back much of his strength, but besides

his prayers, his mind was always somewhere else. Then, one morning in September 2000, he was gone. Mom said he had left in the night, to Bakara market to catch a bus to Baidoa. He told Mom it had rained a lot in Baidoa and he hoped to start farming there. Also, he heard on the radio that the Rahanweyn had learned how to carry guns and had retaken the area. It would be safe for him now. Mom was praying for his safe passage, her forehead on the floor, as Nima made tea.

I think my dad left mainly because he was lost and bored in Mogadishu. There was no work for him, he felt useless. And he had given up on me and Hassan becoming sheikhs. Maybe he could be something in Baidoa. His departure was not the same as when he walked into the bush that night in Baidoa almost ten years before. Now, it was Hassan and I who were the men of the house. He left without even saying goodbye to us, perhaps because he was humiliated.

Of course, I loved my father. However, I was secretly a bit excited that he was gone—first because I hoped he would do better in Baidoa, but also because I knew I would get a break from his harsh scolding about my new lifestyle, from praying with him, and from bathing him and trimming his hair. It was like another freedom to me. None of my friends in Mogadishu even had dads; they had lost theirs in the wars. Mine was alive, and I knew I should be grateful for that. But I also was grateful for more freedom.

Mom had not protested his departure; in fact she encouraged him to leave. It would be less stress for her; she would not worry about him getting shot in Mogadishu. "When your dad settles in Baidoa, we will all move there and start herding animals," she said with a smile. I walked outside and thought, *She is crazy.* I sensed that we would never see Tall Nur again.

I dreaded growing older. Every year, I had watched boys get recruited by militia fighters when they became teenagers. They went from playing soccer and studying the Koran to killing people and chewing qat. Once you enter that life, there is no going back. And if you turn the militias down, they may threaten or kill you. There were so few choices available. You could become a sheikh and call the mosque your home, or you could carry a gun. To me, either was going down a dark path to a world I did not want to live in. My mom did her best. She prayed for our family, for food on our table, for farms and livestock in Baidoa. "Allah has plans for us," she always said.

Meanwhile, Hassan was making his own plans. My brother had returned to the streets after his malaria bout, and he had been hanging out more often at Zobe Square with his friends, sitting against a wall, hiding from the baking sun. I would sit next to them and talk about life.

"I want to leave Somalia," Hassan told me one day.

"You have been saying that for years," I said. "You are still dreaming."

"Now it's for real," he said. "Now I will do it. I have the *buufis.*"

Buufis. That was a word meaning "temptation to leave," and it was being used by young Somalis who had seen all the money coming in from abroad and wanted to get their own life away from Mogadishu.

"Where would you go?" I asked.

"I don't know. Maybe Kenya, Djibouti. But I want to leave Somalia." Young men his age were leaving for Yemen, Kenya, Dubai, Saudi Arabia. These places were by now dealing with so many Somali refugees that it had become a crisis, and they were putting people in refugee camps. Hassan told me that if he left Somalia, he would earn money and send us some, fifty or a hundred dollars a month; that would help our family stay together. These things Hassan told me sounded good, but I did not want him to leave us; we would miss him. In Mogadishu, there was no communication system. If he left, how would we ever stay in touch?

Nearby, a crowd of elderly men were engaged in the regular *fadhi kudirir* debate, a Somali custom where men (never women) gather over tea and talk about clans, politics, animals, and other important topics. They were talking about how great the refugee camps were in Kenya and Yemen. They said the camps were a gateway to America. They bragged of how their kids sent money home. Many were sure they would soon be going to America through something called family sponsorship. But first you had to go through the refugee camps.

"Everyone who is sending money from America had been through those camps," said Hassan. "Once in the camps, it is easy to go to America. It only takes something like three months, and while you wait you get food from the United Nations. It's heaven!"

But without money for transport, Hassan was stuck in Mogadishu. He looked out over the Indian Ocean and asked

Allah for wings to fly across it to America. I told him that beyond the blue waters of the Indian Ocean was heaven. The ocean divided the dead and the living. He laughed at me. "No, Abdi," he said. "There is life beyond the ocean."

I told Hassan how much I missed him at the house, how our family had survived through the wars and the famine, and how we now barely saw each other during the day. How we were all taking separate ways, including our dad. Hassan didn't say much, but I could tell he was also sad.

One morning I went to see him at the wall. Hassan was listening to the elders engage in a heated debate about the new American war in Afghanistan. The men had been cursing the United States. They were organizing protests against the war America started, and against the president. "This is a war between Muslims and non-Muslims," said an elder, throwing one hand in the air as if he wanted to go fight the war himself, while holding a cup of tea in his other hand. The crowd nodded and all said, "Yes!"

I placed one hand on Hassan's shoulder. "Come home, brother," I said.

He did not protest. We walked home together. When I reached out for his hand, he held mine tightly.

Back home, Hassan didn't talk much. When he finally did, he said, "There is life outside Somalia. People who are sending dollars from abroad . . . they left Somalia and now they have jobs."

Mom looked at him.

"Mom, I will leave," he continued. "I need your blessings. We are now grown up, Abdi and me. We can either carry guns and kill people or leave and send money back to our mom and sister." He was right. If I was not enjoying movies and soccer and dancing at weddings, I would be as bored as Hassan and recruited by the militias. I knew that movies and music had saved my life.

I remember Mom looking Hassan in the eyes and saying, "I would like to see you leave. May Allah be with you."

That was all Hassan needed, Mom's prayers. That, and money to get a ride to the border. So we started selling the pigeons Hassan had trained, for a few cents each. We got a total of ten dollars for the birds and two dollars for some wooden scooters that we had built with our own hands.

At dawn on a Sunday morning in September 2004, Hassan walked out the door with twelve dollars and a plastic bag containing a blanket to sleep on.

"Be strong," Mom called from the doorway as we left. "You will make it."

I walked with him and his friend Hussein to Bakara market, to see him off. Again, Hassan and I held hands the same way we had done as children, dodging sniper bullets and rolling jerry cans of water back down. This day we held tighter; I felt like I did not want to let go, but I knew I could not let him stay. He felt the same way. I saw tears in his eyes for the first time in years. Hassan had been strong enough to sleep on the streets of Mogadishu, go a whole day without eating, but it was hard for him to imagine living far away from Mom, Nima, and me. He was on his way out from our family, maybe forever, and we all knew it.

We walked deep inside the dusty market. Then, through

the shouting of the hawkers, we heard our mom's voice coming from behind.

"Hassan! Wait!"

She could not stay home; she'd decided to come say goodbye to her son.

When Hassan saw Mom, tears soaked his face. I watched as my brave mom and brave brother hugged and cried.

"Do you want to change your mind?" she said.

For a minute I thought Hassan would decide to stay, but finally he released Mom and said, "Let's keep walking."

I hugged Mom as we watched the car that would take Hassan to the border of Kenya trundle through a crowd of porters and shoppers, past the market's pyramids of tomatoes and peppers, the driver honking nonstop. Then the car turned, and my brother disappeared.

· 8 ·

WEDDING VOWS

On a burning-hot day in March 2004, me and my friends Bocow and Bashi sat high up in the branches of a neem tree. We were looking out across the city for smoke. Where there was smoke, there was food, and we were very hungry. Then we saw it: a big fire, lots of people. Probably an arranged wedding. We climbed down, grabbed our boom box, and crashed that party. Time for some food and dancing!

With more money and more men in the city, weddings were happening almost every week in Mogadishu, with cow meat, camel milk, fruits, and dance music. Except for very strict Muslims (who had not yet taken over the city), a wedding without dancing is considered incomplete for Somalis. But most of the traditional Somali musicians had been killed or had fled during the fighting, so there was no live music; you had to use a boom box and cassette tapes.

People with a lot of cassette tapes were in demand for weddings, especially if they also knew how to dance and could get the party going.

About once a week I would get hailed on the street to perform at a wedding. People yelled my new name, Abdi American, at every corner of my neighborhood when I passed. I would show up with my group of dancers and play music for the crowd. After one wedding, the bride's dad gave me a few American dollars, the first I had ever held in my hand. It was enough to buy maize and camel milk for my family. Not everyone could pay me to dance, and usually I did it for free. Most important, I got a reputation. Girls would come to my house, walking past Mom and Aunt Dhuha into my room just to chat and flirt with me. When I was out, Mom told me girls she didn't even know were coming to our house, asking for me. And wherever I went to dance, girls came, watched, and clapped. When I walked on the streets, girls shouted, "Abdi American!" I just waved and moved on.

One afternoon we walked into a wedding celebration, dressed in our usual California street gang attire of head wraps, plastic bracelets, baggy jeans, and hats. I set up my boom box and played my latest tape, brand-new to Mogadishu: "In da Club" by 50 Cent. People loved this new song. Then a beautiful girl stepped onto the dance floor. She had a big smile, and her dark brown braided hair flowed down her neck from under her head scarf. She was wearing an orange *dirac*, or traditional dress, in a *maqbal* pattern of brilliant flowers. She coyly swayed, covering her face with her colorfully painted hands. This girl obviously did not know how to dance, but I thought she was so brave to be the first to try. Some of the wedding guests cheered her, but others booed. Another girl in the crowd yelled, "Stupid girl, sit down!"

She leaned in to my ear to say something.

"I can't dance," she said.

"I can teach you," I said. "What's your name?"

"Faisa."

Then the girl who had been scolding her jumped onto the dance floor, grabbed Faisa by the hand, and dragged her outside the building, yelling at her. "I will tell Dad, I will tell Dad!" she screamed. So they were sisters.

I would soon learn that their dad was Sheikh Omar, an important cleric in the Waberi neighborhood. He led the five daily prayers at the mosque, and also the important Friday prayers. Sheikh Omar was also a judge mediating divorce, marriage, and child support cases according to the Koran, which he knew not just in Arabic but also in Somali. Fortunately, he was too busy to pay much attention to his daughters, which is why Faisa and her sister could dress up and go to weddings where dance music was played. But listening was one thing. Dancing was another.

I went outside to look for Faisa, leaving the wedding party behind. I found her sitting by herself, fanning her face against the late afternoon heat.

"*Asalaamu aleikum,*" I greeted her. Peace be upon you.

"*Wa'aleikum salaam,*" she replied. And unto you, peace.

She stood up, smiled, and said she was happy to see me.

I was so nervous. She told me she had to go home before sunset, and it was already five o'clock.

"I want to see you again," I said.

"Okay," she said, offering to meet up the next day and adding that she hoped I could teach her to dance.

"Could you come to Aargada Arch tomorrow at four o'clock?" I asked.

I knew I would not be able to teach her to dance, because we had no private place to hang out. She would never come to our house, because her dad would never allow it, and Omar would certainly not invite me to their house. And in Mogadishu, even what happens inside is not private; everything can be heard behind tin or mud walls. A boy and a girl cannot date; only marriage is allowed. What Faisa and I wanted to do was unusual. Still, we could try.

The next day, Faisa appeared, walking down Maka al-Mukarama Street with a smile, looking happy to see me. We walked side by side, enjoying a cool breeze from the sea. I could not take her to a tea shop or a restaurant; all I could do was take her to Hamarweyne for a walk through the old part of Mogadishu, down the streets with coconut trees on each side and the Indian Ocean beyond. I talked to her about my dad's basketball games, how life had been good for us before the war. She talked about how they had fled to Ethiopia in 1991, then returned to Mogadishu six years later. Now she was curious about the music I had played at the wedding. "How did they create such a sweet thing?" she asked. "Where do those people live?"

I told her they live in America, the same place as my nickname. She started calling me Abdi American.

Our next meeting was the day before Ramadan. She had prepared *bajiyas* and samosas specially for me. We walked again down the street, me taking bites of the *bajiya* as Faisa talked about her family. Her story was interrupted by a group of hungry street kids who had followed the smell of the fresh snacks and begged for some. I gave everything to them.

Faisa looked me in the eye and said, "You are so generous."

I told her that the kids reminded me of my childhood, when hunger was an enemy that can make you eat anything. There was no way I could not give it to them.

We talked about fun things we could try to do together, like go to Uruba beach. This war had gone on for thirteen years, and we were so sick of it. We wanted lives. I already danced on the streets and spoke English; why not go to the beach with my girl? I knew the dangers that could come from bringing a girl to such a public place, though. There were boys in militias who had been raised in the war and thought assaulting girls was fun. So I organized my posse of friends as bodyguards as I walked with Faisa. It didn't take long for crowds to gather and stare at us.

Faisa trusted in me and stayed very close to my side as she waded into the ocean in her clothes. Every time I saw guys moving close to her in the water, I jumped up and used my best Mogadishu gangster dialect to shout, "Stay away!" I even added an f-bomb for effect. I had perfected a good Mogadishu accent, so everyone thought I was from the Hawiye tribe and probably had militia connections. It was Faisa's first time in the ocean, and whenever the waves rolled in toward us, she would race back to the shore in terror, like she was being chased. But her shock turned to excitement. Going to the beach would become our favorite thing to do. I would write her name on my arm with a piece of charcoal, like a tattoo. She wrote my name on her arm too, but she always made sure the ocean had erased it before she went home.

Then, one day, Faisa's father, Sheikh Omar, found out that I would sometimes hang out by her window. He went straight to my house to yell at my mother. "If you can't stop this boy from stalking our girl, we will take measures against him!" Then he stormed off.

When I came home that evening, Mom was waiting for me at the door. She was so angry that she hit me with a broom, then with her sandals. "Stay away from Faisa!" she shouted. "Her dad came here threatening me!"

Soon my relationship with Faisa was known on every corner in the neighborhood. Weeks passed and there was no sight of her until, one day, while she was at the market buying bananas and tomatoes, I ran into her.

We agreed to meet up in secret at Aargada Arch again, while her parents were out of town. She and her sisters needed to welcome their parents back with fresh food. She had been told by her sisters to go gather fruits in Afgooye.

Afgooye was the same part of Somalia where I had seen

the scary blue monkeys as a little boy fleeing to Baidoa. The bus ride over brought back terrible memories. This time the road was different. There were still roadblocks where militias robbed travelers, but it was not as terrifying as the last time. When the bus arrived, I felt relieved to see Faisa. Together, we collected papayas, mangoes, and bananas hanging from the trees. The only sounds we heard were the splashes of the crocodiles and the squealing of the monkeys jumping from tree to tree.

"Faisa, I want to kiss you," I said after we had finished her fruit errand. My heart was beating so fast as I waited for an answer. She coyly giggled. I came close and gave her a quick peck on the cheek. Her skin was soft and she smelled like heaven. Kissing Faisa on the cheek that day was a moment in my life that I will never forget. First kiss, first time. She told me I would have to wait until the day of our marriage for the next one.

"When will that be?" I asked.

"I don't know," she said. "Only Allah knows."

It was not impossible for a Hawiye girl to marry a Rahanweyn boy, but it would have been very hard. In fact, after our getaway to Afgooye, it would be a long time before I saw Faisa again.

●●●

Someone returned from Kenya who had seen Hassan in the refugee camps in Wajeer, which our dad's sister Amina had also reached. This person carried a letter to me from Hassan. It was handwritten in English.

Abdi it is Hassan I am doing well. I am in Wa-
jeer Kenya. Our car broke down somewhere near
the border with Kenya and I had to walk three
days to get to the border. I met lions and hyenas on
the streets, scary and remembered Mom's stories.
Anyway, everything is good with me. I am trying
to get to Nairobi. The refugee camp here in Wajeer
is very hard, really tough like Somalia people are
dying from hunger. I heard Nairobi is a good place
that I can work at least. Abdi there is something
called Hotmail. You can create an account on the
internet, create one and lets talk there and my
hotmail address is hansiftin@hotmail.com. Say
hi to Mom and Nima.

Life was so different with both Hassan and Dad gone.
When I came home at night after watching a movie, the
house was dead quiet. Hassan and I had used to stay up,
chatting in English. Now I was all by myself, lonely and
bored. Nima was now fourteen and had been practicing
her regular daily chores starting from dawn. She did not
have friends like me; her only companion was Mom. Nima
was tall, and like every other girl in the city, she had been
putting on eyeliner, coloring her nails, and putting henna
tattoos on her hands. After Hassan left, Nima and I grew
closer; we entertained each other at home playing *gariir*
and hopscotch.

One afternoon some strange guests came to visit. They
were five men all dressed in long white robes. Mom of-

fered them seats on the floor. One was about thirty years old and introduced himself as Omar. He scowled at me in my Western-style clothes. Mom asked Nima to prepare tea for them. I was on my way to a movie and snuck past Mom while she and the men were talking. To my surprise, when I came back that evening, the guests were still there, all eating meat and maize.

As I came in, the man called Omar scowled at me again, but then he reached into his pocket, pushed aside his beard comb and mirror, and pulled out five American dollar bills. After he was sure we could all see his money, he gave me one of the bills and said, "It is yours." It turned out Omar had a cousin in America who was sending him fifty dollars a month.

I was still confused why they were here and why they were giving me the money. But in Somali culture, it is not appropriate to ask guests questions like that. I went to Nima, who was making tea behind a curtain we used to separate our house from the kitchen. "Who are these people?" I whispered.

"I was about to ask you," she said.

From the kitchen, we overheard them talking about a wedding, presents of goats, a silent Muslim ceremony with no dancing. Omar was explaining his plan, saying it would happen on Thursday.

"Nima, come here," said Mom. Nima came running from the kitchen. "Look how gorgeous she looks!" Mom said to the men. "Nima, you are so lucky. Omar has come to marry you. And we accepted."

Nima had no words; I think she almost had a heart attack. Of course she knew she would someday be married, but she never expected to marry a man more than twice her age whom she had never met. I was in just as much shock, and I felt so betrayed that our mom would do this with no conversation, just a trade-off for some money and goats.

Mom told us that Omar just got in from Baidoa and that he was Rahanweyn. Mom said it was actually our dad, through a messenger sent to Dhuha, who made the decision to marry Nima to Omar. The culture did not allow Mom to disagree. The wedding was happening next Thursday, and two goats would be slaughtered. Guests including Macalin Basbaas had been invited; there would be sheikhs present, which meant no music or fun at all. Just eating meat and praying.

Mom talked about how fortunate Nima was to marry a man who had memorized the Koran, who regularly went to the mosque, who never missed praying five times a day, and who received money from abroad. "Nima, look at you! You are so lucky!" Mom said.

Nima was still out of breath and could say nothing.

• • •

The wedding day came. It would be Nima's last day in our house, leaving me home all alone with Mom. But I wasn't feeling sorry for myself, only for Nima. She was terrified.

That morning we cut goat meat into small cubes and put a huge pot of maize on the wood fire. By early Thursday morning, neighbors and religious leaders, including Macalin

Basbaas, were sitting peacefully under the shade of a tree, murmuring the Koran and feasting on the meat, milk, and maize. I served them water to wash their hands. The droning of the prayers and the eating went on for hours. Because it was a strict religious wedding, Nima was forced to wear a heavy traditional dark hijab. She sat there baking in the sun, breathing heavily.

After it all, Mom and I walked Nima down to her new house, six blocks away. I hugged her goodbye. She cried. Mom gave her some final marriage advice: "Be obedient."

I whispered in her ear some different advice: "Don't allow him to restrict you. Come home whenever you can."

With Nima married, Mom was lonely and decided to journey to Baidoa and search for my dad, who had been gone for a year. She set off on the Afgooye road by bus and arrived in Baidoa two days later.

Baidoa was very different from the last time she saw it, during our escape from Mogadishu. She walked through stall after stall in the market. Giant slabs of red meat were swinging in the sunlight. In other stalls, people sold long strips of dried meat called *kalaankal*, which was chopped into small pieces and fried. In the grain market, women sold every variety of corn and seeds from sacks that attracted bees, wasps, and flies. Vegetables, watermelons, papayas, and bananas, all grown nearby, were everywhere. Men who were pushing wheelbarrows ran to Mom, offering their services. Streets and open spaces were crammed with chickens, mattresses, shoes, and bright fabrics. And everyone spoke her Maay language.

Mom sat down on a rock near a kiosk that was selling freshly squeezed fruits and ordered a glass of mango juice to cool herself after walking in the hot sun. She scanned her eyes through the crowd to see if our dad was somewhere around there. She asked people if they knew Nur Dhere. No one knew. But then she remembered she needed to say Nur Dhere in Maay, which would be Nurey. She had lived in Mogadishu for so long she forgot to use her native tongue.

"Do you know Nurey, the tall guy?" she asked a woman.

The lady said yes. She said our dad could be found working in the charcoal market. Mom walked down to the charcoal market, a filthy place where the air was black with charcoal dust.

"Nurey!" she cried.

Within minutes he emerged from the dust like a ghost, covered head to toe in soot. They walked back to his battered tin kiosk, surrounded with bags of charcoal. A little boy, named Deeq, was sitting in the soot drinking camel milk. Dad explained that Deeq was one of his two children with his new wife. She was dark and thin, ten years younger than he, and she sold tea next to his charcoal business.

In Somali culture, a man can marry up to four wives. Mom was respectful and told him that she missed his presence. He cursed Mogadishu as a place of the devil. Then she said goodbye.

· 9 ·

SIN AND PUNISHMENT

By early 2005, Somalia had a new, transitional government for the first time since the civil war started. But this government was based abroad, in Kenya. Politicians were staying away because the warlords, with their thousands of militiamen, were still in charge of Mogadishu. The new government had given the warlords ministerial positions in the hope they would be cooperative and back down. But the warlords had no intention of giving up control. They were making millions of dollars in ransom by pirating merchant ships off the coast. Then they found a source for even more money.

The U.S. government believed that some of the terrorists who had bombed an American embassy in Nairobi in 1998 were hiding in Somalia. And the government knew that the Hawiye warlords had the power to find and capture terrorists. Soon the warlords—the same groups that had brought down the two Black Hawk helicopters and dragged the bodies of U.S. troops through the streets of Mogadishu—were helping the U.S. government hunt down potential terrorists.

Of course the Americans didn't publicize this new partnership. The warlords were happy to make it known, though. In fact, everyone could see that they were now swimming in money while raiding mosques and grabbing radical sheikhs. This began a massive purge of not just potential terrorists but of men who were Islamic scholars and madrassa teachers, who were abducted, deported, and "disappeared." The warlords grew bolder by the day, turning the hunt for terrorists into a reign of terror—culminating in the shocking assassination of the chairman of the Ifka Halane Islamic Court.

Here's where the politics become a little complicated. At that time, there were five Islamic courts in Mogadishu, each corresponding to a clan. Without a government, the courts settled cases and disagreements, everything from divorces to petty crimes. Mostly they ordered payments of animals or cash; there was no corporal punishment, and they had no armed enforcers. The Ifka Halane Court chairman was a popular man. He was also a Hawiye, the same clan as the warlords and most residents of Mogadishu, which is what made his killing such a shock. In mosques across Mogadishu, the assassination inspired tirades against both the violent warlords and their American supporters. Public opinion quickly turned even further against the warlords.

This shift became an opportunity for the five Islamic courts to unite, despite their clan differences, against a common enemy. They soon gained the support of the Hawiye people, which made it even harder for the Hawiye warlords to claim leadership. People in Mogadishu were tired of lawlessness, tired of warlords, tired of attacks on their religion. The world's war on terrorism since 9/11 had become perceived in Mogadishu as a war on Islam. This in turn boosted public support for the Islamic courts and against the Western-backed warlords. When the courts banded together, calling themselves the Islamic Courts Union (ICU), the stage was set for a radical Islamic takeover.

The first chairman of the ICU was Sheikh Sharif Ahmed. He was a madrassa teacher who brought together a group of his students and other young men to train for a war against the warlords. Even though he was Hawiye himself, he reached out to other tribes including my own, the Rahanweyn. Everything he said was based on the Koran and strict Sharia law. Every time he talked, he cursed the United States and its allies, like Ethiopia. People in Mogadishu who were furious at the Islamophobia of the West found a man they could listen to.

Soon the ICU established a unified Sharia legal system throughout Mogadishu, as opposed to the earlier courts, which were independent and unorganized. It trained its own well-disciplined magistrates, young men with shaved heads and long beards, to settle cases of theft, forgery, rape, and divorce, all based on the Koran. Secretly, they were also training young men as Islamic soldiers, practicing with weapons outside the city late at night. With enough training, they believed, they could form a religious army that could fight against the warlords. But first they began killing anyone who resisted Islamic law.

By now the wealthier members of the Hawiye clan were contributing money to the ICU, which enabled the Islamists to buy more arms and attract more young soldiers. Soon they had taken over the important seaport of El Ma'an, just north of Mogadishu. Following that takeover, a series of clashes between the ICU militias and the warlord militias brought Islamic control over several neighborhoods right in Mogadishu. Besides strict Sharia law, the ICU restored security and provided social services and charitable works. People were happy to find fresh water available and police on the streets. This popular support for the ICU motivated the religious militias to face the warlords in other areas of Mogadishu, which started months of bitter battles across the city.

The ICU launched a massive recruitment effort. It held huge demonstrations all over town, where speakers preached of the holy mission and the rewards of the afterlife for Islamic martyrs. Young men in Mogadishu who had no jobs, no future, and nothing to do hurried to sign up to go to heaven in the name of Allah. They did not fear death. In fact, the promise of an afterlife in paradise was appealing.

By April 2006, most of Mogadishu was under the control of the ICU, and the warlords had scattered. Clans didn't matter anymore, only Allah. I was walking in places where

I once dodged bullets, places gangs and militias had ruled, now without fear. The city was different. One flag, the color black with a white script that said "There is no god but God himself," was flying everywhere. The houses were still in ruins, but Mogadishu felt reborn. People started volunteering for civic duties such as clearing the rubbish from the streets, rebuilding houses, and opening the airport that had been closed for sixteen years. Instead of gunshots constantly, we heard Islamic chants blaring from huge speakers on the trucks of the ICU fighters. Mosques were filled with people who again felt the freedom to worship without fear of being abducted by warlords. After prayers, the sheikhs would curse America and praise Osama bin Laden. *America is the enemy of Allah, God bless Osama inshallah.*

Life *seemed* peaceful. The Islamists were doing a good job by not allowing bullying or clan superiority, and by kicking out the militias. If anyone bullied anyone else under their rule, you could call out for help and an enforcer would show up, like calling 911 in America. But to me, the Islamists were not in Mogadishu to scrve and protect, they were here to deprive me of my freedoms. The ICU had announced a curfew from dusk to dawn. Anyone seen on the street was assumed to be breaking the law and could be imprisoned or shot. I was not sure what to do with the new changes in the city.

Among the people happy for the change in Mogadishu, though, was my mom, who had opened a kiosk in Bakara market where she sold maize, sorghum, and rice. I helped her out in the market, trying to make us some money. When she wasn't working, Mom went to ICU-run workshops. Many were on the subject of death, killing, and Sharia law. Mom got an Islamic flag and flew it over our house. I could not remove it, because houses without the flag would be targeted.

One day Mom came to me and suggested I join the Islamists. "They are going to be rich," she said. "There is no other faith but Islam; they will conquer the whole world! They are acting on the Sharia!"

"Mom, I want to be who I am. I can't carry guns and shoot at people."

At night, when the air cooled down, everyone was forced to go to former soccer fields and watch young Islamists train for battle. It was like U.S. Marines boot camp—strenuous fitness drills, foot marching, training exercises, and weapons use. I was bored and wanted to leave, but attendance was mandatory. When it finally ended, the soldiers prayed not for peace but for war with America and Europe: "God, make us meet American troops, make us wipe them out. Give us the upper hand. We are your soldiers."

These events lured thousands more young men to sign up for what I always called "the one-way ticket." But they were too late to get me. I didn't want to die for them; I wanted to live in a beautiful American city. Every day I wondered if the world knew what was happening in Mogadishu. At times I was mad at America for leaving us behind in 1994. Would anyone save us now?

. . .

Every day, my heart pounded with the fear of being recruited as a soldier for the Islamists. I knew that once you joined, there was no return. You could not decide to drop your gun and be a normal person again. Death was the only way out, and death was calling to everyone my age.

Friends who had once played soccer with me were joining the Islamists. Guys I had laughed with at Eddie Murphy movies now signed up for the holy war. The training grounds in Mogadishu were thronged with these young men and women, all fighting for the title *jihadi*, or for *shaheed*, a martyr. They had been instructed to fight sin. And sin included sports, movies, music, Western clothes, even the way we walked and talked.

One of the new recruits was Mukhtar, a boy I had gone to madrassa with. He graduated after me, then became an assistant to Macalin Basbaas, who of course was happy with the Islamists. Mukhtar and I played soccer together before the Islamists came, but now he had changed. His name was now Abu Jihad. He had been told by his emir to go eliminate sin, so naturally he thought of me.

One afternoon, he and a fellow Islamist came to my home, saying they were looking around for anything sinful. Abu Jihad saw my Western-style jeans and cap hanging on a peg. He ripped them off the wall and slashed them with his knife. He searched through the room and found my boom box. He knew I used it to play tapes and dance at weddings; he knew everything I did. He turned to his *jihadi* friend and said, "Look at this sin!" Using their gun butts, they smashed the boom box to pieces before my eyes.

"We have our eyes on you!" said Abu Jihad. Then he left. That same night, worried about all the threats in the city, Falis removed all the movie posters from the video shack. She hid the tiny television in her bedroom.

Through all of this turmoil, life had to go on, and we soon got word that my sister, Nima, was pregnant with her first baby. I had not seen Nima in several months, but we heard that she was in much pain.

When I visited the tiny room she shared with her husband, Omar, she told me she had been in bed, pregnant, for weeks. Her body was covered with rashes and pimples. Her skin was darker. Even as sick as she was, carrying a baby, Nima had to cook for her husband so that he could be fed when he came home at sunset. It was hard for her with all the pain. I went back many times to help her cook, clean, and wash, each time seeking permission from Omar first. Nima had her baby, a healthy girl, but my sister never fully recovered.

At least I had some good news from my brother: Hassan had made it to Nairobi. It turned out the refugee camps were no paradise on earth. They were violent, filthy, and hopeless places, where the same militias and gangs of Mogadishu terrorized people.

Through our emails, Hassan was the only person left in my world who encouraged me to keep up my American dream. The Internet café in Bakara market had not been closed by the Islamists, because they also used it. Hassan emailed in English so the Islamists couldn't read his words. Of course that was dangerous too, because if anyone saw me reading English, they would surely find a way to translate—maybe even execute me for praising America.

During this time, Abu Jihad kept his word, checking on me daily. When I saw him approach our gate, I would sneak out the back, avoiding him. I would spend time with my mom in the market, then after sunset I would sneak back into the house. Nights were so scary. I could hear the murmurs and conversations of the Islamist soldiers outside the mud walls of my room, and I could hear the screams of people they were beating for minor mistakes, or any behavior that wasn't accepted by Sharia law.

One night two bombs exploded in Falis's video shack. The first one pierced the roof; the second destroyed the television in her bedroom, and the cassettes. When we all woke up in the morning, we learned Falis had been taken to prison by a group of Islamists. I ran to the shack. A crowd built up as I stood there watching my beloved video shack disappear before my eyes. This, not the dreaded madrassa, had been my real school. The ICU had brought in a bulldozer, which was clearing the rubble of the explosion. A group of young fighters gathered. They said the land had been found to be sinful and therefore it should be turned into a preaching place where people would be taught Islamic lessons. A fighter walked up to the crowd, holding the Koran in his right hand, talking about how sinful it is to watch movies. "Wherever you see sin, you must destroy it with your hands!"

Soccer, movies, music, dancing—these were all the things that had kept me going in Mogadishu. Now, with everything banned, my future was falling into a deep dark hole. I started writing to Hassan only once every two weeks, always in Somali. One day I emailed him, "I don't know if I will be able to email you again, but, Hassan, in case you don't hear from me, I might be in the hands of the Terminators." That was our secret word for the Islamists.

"I think my world is going to end soon," I wrote. "Mom wants me to join the ICU. I am scared of carrying a gun. I want to leave."

Hassan wrote back, "Abdi, these Islamists will be like the Taliban. I think America will do air strikes against them. I am scared for you too. Let's think of a way for you to leave."

· 10 ·

TRAPPED

One Thursday morning in June 2006, when I was about twenty-one, Faisa came over to see me. She had snuck out of her family's home. I had not seen her for months. Underneath her hijab, I could see her bright orange *dirac* and a shawl. She looked me in the eyes and said, "I've missed you. Take us somewhere."

I did not know where to take her; the city had changed so much since she and I used to walk together. At that moment, the streets were clear, but there were so many Islamist checkpoints in the city. We both knew that men and women walking together was considered a crime now. But we didn't know the punishment. My heart was beating hard as I looked down the street in case the Islamists returned.

The only place I could think of for us to go was Uruba beach, our old meeting place a few miles away. Walking that far with an unrelated woman would be way too dangerous, so we took a minibus, sitting separately. As we approached the beach, Faisa kept a few steps behind me. We did not talk to each other, but I constantly looked behind to make sure she was okay. When we got up to Bank Street, overlooking the green water of the Indian Ocean, we each inhaled the fresh sea air.

People were crowded on the beach, but not for fun or relaxation. Most were washing their clothes in the seawater, or fishing. None of the women dared to get into the water. Except Faisa. She stood in the sand and removed her face cover, gloves, sandals, then her socks and her heavy hijab. "I was choking to death in these clothes!" she said. I smiled and told her about how people in Miami and California go to beaches just for fun, wearing bikinis and shorts. I told her that if we were in Miami, we would see white sailboats out across the water, more people having fun on those boats. We were laughing, talking, and happily splashing. But this was Mogadishu. It didn't take long for the crowd to spot us and start complaining. Women yelled out to Faisa, shaming her for removing her hijab.

Faisa felt so humiliated. We quickly got out, but someone had already run down the road and called the Islamists. Before we had even dried off, four angry teenage boys with covered faces, guns on their shoulders, and whips in their hands surrounded us. Without saying anything, they just started flogging us with their whips. One guy whipped Faisa; two others knocked me to the sand and pressed their rubber sandals against my face, while a third whipped me viciously. Faisa was screaming, "I will not do it again!"

One of the enforcers pointed at her wet body, barely concealed under her clinging wet *dirac*, and yelled repeatedly, "What is this? *What is this?* Is this Europe? Or America? What are you wearing?"

Then he turned to me. "Who allowed you to walk with a girl holding hands?"

A crowd had gathered around to watch the drama unfold. I could hear people murmuring, "He's the *American* guy." They laughed and said I was stupid. Then Faisa and I, bleeding from our wounds, were marched down the next block into an old building next to the former National Bank of Somalia. This was a makeshift prison and court where people caught in different criminal activities were taken. Faisa was accused of breaking Sharia law. Two men led her into a room and closed the door.

Finally, I was brought into a small room. I was made to get on my knees before an interrogator, who asked me my name, where I lived, and what I did for a living. "My name is Abdi, I live in KM4, I don't do anything."

He scribbled my information in Arabic on a sheet of paper, walked away, and came back with the magistrate, who was scowling. He opened a Koran and read, "Tell the believing men to lower their gaze, and protect their private parts . . . and tell the believing women to lower their gaze, and protect their private parts."

Of course I knew that verse. I knew the whole Koran

by heart, but today for the first time, I was seeing it used directly against me. My punishment was twenty lashes and "counseling." I wasn't sure what "counseling" meant. I knew what twenty lashes meant. A man whose face was obscured under a thick beard came before me with a huge leather whip. He started flogging me as he counted down the lashes: "Twenty . . . nineteen . . . eighteen . . ." When the lash hit my skin, it was like being stabbed repeatedly with needles.

After the whipping, my "counseling" began. Same guy; he just set down his whip and quizzed me on the Koran. "What are the names of the prophets? Recite the ninety-nine names of Allah!" On and on. When they finally let us go, they warned us we would receive more counseling later at the mosque.

Faisa was lashed as well, then sent home with a warning that if they saw her going to the beach again, she would regret it for the rest of her life. I never showed up at the mosque. Friday prayers were a time of massive recruitment for the holy war, and I suspected my counseling would be a trap to enlist me. I knew that if I were to avoid the recruiters, I had to blend in. My jeans and cap had already been slashed by my old soccer pal Mukhtar. Now I stopped speaking English, dancing, and playing soccer. Falis's video shack was gone; the movies were gone. Everything fun was gone. Even my meager source of income was lost, because it was no longer safe to teach English. I canceled classes.

· 11 ·

NO NUMBER

Hassan was right. By July 2006, the United States–supported Ethiopian army was slowly advancing toward Mogadishu to drive out the Islamists, while I was trying to escape. Finally they crossed over with tens of thousands of well-trained soldiers, backed by tanks and airplanes.

A week after the war broke out, Ethiopian troops marched into Mogadishu. Now it was my turn to be happy. I walked through the streets for hours with no signs of an Islamist. All that remained were their black flags, snapping in the fresh breeze.

On New Year's Day 2007, the sun rose above the blue flag of Somalia, flying for the first time in years.

The foreign peacekeeping troops that poured into Mogadishu from Ethiopia and the African Union did not understand Somalia's complex history and clan rivalries.

They didn't realize how the majority Hawiye clan of the city would resent the new American- and Ethiopian-sponsored Darod president and fear all the Darod soldiers now swarming into Mogadishu. When the civil war started in 1991, the Hawiye militias had killed thousands of Darods and then invaded the Rahanweyn land. Hawiye civilians wondered whether these Darod and Rahanweyn soldiers would now take revenge on them. When the order came down to disarm the city, the Hawiye—once the aggressors—now felt threatened and vulnerable.

It didn't take long for the Hawiye elders to declare Ethiopia nothing more than an occupying army. "We kicked America out!" they said. "It won't take us long to defeat you!"

The call from the elders became an opportunity for the Islamists to regroup and launch a holy war. This time, with the enemy right in their midst, it became guerrilla warfare. Suicide bombers targeted government buildings. Masked assassins killed anyone even remotely suspected of helping the Ethiopians and the new government. These newly radicalized Islamists called themselves al-Shabaab, "the Youth."

With the clash of international armies and the suicide bombings, the world was again paying attention to Somalia. But very few international journalists would risk coming. One who did was Paul Salopek, a Pulitzer Prize–winning reporter then with the *Chicago Tribune*.

Here's how we met. One day I was walking through town, when I heard the click and whir of a motorized camera from a building across the street. Cameras were not normal sounds in Mogadishu. Up on the balcony of a guesthouse was an Asian photographer and a white man. The white guy waved. I waved back. Then his bodyguards, some hired Somali militiamen at the gate of the house, thought I was making trouble for them. They pointed their AK-47s at my head.

"Go away!" said one. "Leave *now*."

I was so afraid I would be shot, but I summoned all my courage and yelled up at the white guy. "I want to talk to you!" I said in my best English.

The man disappeared inside. The militiamen were getting angrier, shaking their guns.

"He is okay. Let him come." The voice from the courtyard was in English. It was the white man, now at the gate. Then we shook hands. He introduced himself as a journalist.

"Hi," I said. "It is good to meet you, sir. I am very excited!"

When he heard me speak English, Paul's eyebrows went up. "Wow! Come on up, man."

Then he asked, "What do you drink, hot or cold?" We were on his balcony. He had a Pepsi in one hand, and a kettle of tea was on the table. I never had Pepsi in my life. I only saw it in movies.

"That one," I said, pointing to the Pepsi.

"What's your name?"

"My name is Abdi."

"Abdi. Are you from this area?"

"Yes, I live down that road, toward the big tree over there." I pointed down in the direction of our house. I took a sip of the Pepsi. It tasted cold and delicious.

Paul asked me a lot of questions about life in Mogadishu, and I told him my story. He and Kuni Takahashi, his Japanese-born photographer, were surprised that I had learned English just from watching movies. I told them how most guys my age had been recruited by the Islamists, and I felt my luck was running out. "It sucks to be here, man," I said, using my best Hollywood slang.

Then I started asking Paul questions about America. New York, California, the cars, the food, what snow is like. Paul soon realized how much I loved America, and he said something that gave me hope.

"Abdi, I am sure that one day you will live in America." We spoke for three hours. When I left, Paul handed me his business card. Then he reached into his pocket and pulled out fifty dollars.

"Here, buy a cell phone so I can call you. What's left, give to your family." By now, cheap cell phones were becoming widely available in Somalia.

We hugged and waved goodbye.

"Abdi," said Paul from the gate. "Make sure you email me your phone number."

• • •

Walking out of that building was a return to the apocalypse. No more English, no more Pepsi. I might have been killed for meeting a white man. Thankfully, nobody had seen us, so I tucked the fifty dollars underneath my belt and headed directly to the cell phone store.

Just before I reached the store, a bomb went off in front of it. As I ducked for cover, another exploded nearby. Suicide bombers were hitting Ethiopian troops right on that road. Gunfire erupted all over, and I ran. People all around me ran. Night fell, and the hellfire rained down over town. I had never seen Mogadishu's sky turn red like that before. It felt like the entire earth was cracking in half.

When the bombing stopped the next day, life returned on the streets. I walked into the nearby cybercafé and emailed Paul: "Dear Paul. I hope you are okay. I just came out of hiding from the shelling and the bombing. I am safe and will buy a phone soon so that we can communicate. Best wishes. Abdi."

Paul emailed me back a minute later: "Hey Abdi. My friend, you are such a strong man. I am glad I met you. Let's continue talking. Meanwhile, stay safe. P."

That was getting harder and harder. By now, the citizens of Mogadishu were trapped between al-Shabaab and the government forces. The morning after the big attack, Mom and I went to her stall to find that her small business had been reduced to a smoking pile of burnt grain bags. Probably one of the Ethiopian rockets had hit it during the night.

Before we could flee the market, the battle erupted again. Mom pointed to the nearby mosque and yelled that we should go inside. She didn't think it would be any safer, only that if we died in there, it would be our ticket to heaven. Almost a hundred people had already squeezed inside the brick sanctuary, reading the Koran, crying, and calling out names of family members who were missing. Some people had cell phones and were calling relatives. Of course mosques have minarets (tall slender towers used for the Muslim call to prayer), which make good sniper posts, and soon al-Shabaab soldiers were climbing the towers and shooting from the high windows at the advancing Ethiopians. When the foreign tanks found their way to the mosque, the first hit destroyed one of the minarets, sending bricks and rubble raining down. Before the second round could come, Mom and I decided against dying in the mosque and dashed out, holding hands. We ran and ran, not sure where we were going, but we followed a crowd that was heading south toward the Thirty Road.

Rockets being fired from the tanks landed all around us. Bullets whistled. One time I looked behind me, and the building we had just passed seconds ago was now flattened. But in front of us were al-Shabaab fighters, unafraid of dying and wrapped in suicide bombs. *Now what?* We could not go home. All roads going that way were blocked by the shelling.

"This way," I said, pointing down a road with no explosions. But before we got more than a few steps, an Ethiopian helicopter gunship swooped down like a space alien and opened fire. I could see dust flying off the ground, people falling, blood spilling.

Even more people had joined us, fleeing for their safety. We all hurried away, down a narrow alley that led out to a street and from there to an open space of small hills and sand dunes. By now, we were miles away from the city and its bombs, walking deep into al-Shabaab territory. Mom and I joined hundreds of other displaced people who were building huts from sticks and cardboard. I came across bones and a skull as I set to work building a hut. I used what I could find of trash and sticks to make a shelter that was barely big enough to protect my mom from blowing dust. She slept in there that night, me just outside.

By the next day, the camp was crowded with makeshift huts people had built with whatever was lying around. It all happened so quickly and, unfortunately, the people of Mogadishu had a lot of experience adapting to violence and being on the run. Sunrise revealed the faces of hundreds that had been walking all night long, tired faces and hungry mouths. Incredibly, among these hundreds of hungry people, we ran into my sister, Nima, and her baby daughter, Mumira. It was our family reunion. Nima's husband, Omar, was nowhere to be seen. He had disappeared into the city, maybe dead or alive.

The new camp was named Eelasha, which means "water." During the days of the Somali government, this place had wells that provided water throughout Mogadishu. In the civil war, everything was looted and the wells were buried. Now there was only the name to torment thirsty people.

Within a week, business activities had sprung up in the camp. Everything that was in Bakara market moved to Eelasha. The money-transfer agencies, telephone companies, mosques, everything. Macalin Basbaas had even built a hut for his new madrassa. Dhuha and her kids also moved in. It had become its own city. New friends, new neighbors, new Koranic teachers, and a new administration: the Harakat al-Shabaab al-Mujahedeen. Al-Shabaab fighters called on all men to gather at the mosque five times a day.

We were told that the Mujahedeen needed more men to fight for them. My heart was in my throat. Many times I had been able to avoid recruitment by slipping off and losing myself in the streets of Mogadishu. Out here in the camp, there was no place to hide. Soon enough, I was ordered to report for training.

We gathered under a tree, new recruits. We were told to call the government the *Murtadeen*, the apostates. "The president, the prime minister, cabinet members, and everyone else involved are all non-Muslims, enemies of Allah," said a young teenager who still had a boy's voice and face. "They should be killed the same way we should kill Americans and Europeans."

A man dressed in a military vest with a long kanzu and a beard started our training—how to wear an explosive vest, how to approach the enemy, then how to shoot people.

By the end of the day, I felt sick.

That night I whispered to my mom, "Mom, I have to go back to Mogadishu. I'm leaving now." In the paper huts we were staying in, al-Shabaab could hear even whispers, so Mom said nothing but just brushed her hands on mine. Creeping out of the hut, I tried not to make a sound. I swiftly walked in the dark up over the Kaxda hills and across the open bush, trying to avoid the trails where al-Shabaab had planted land mines in case of attack. By three in the morning I had made it back to our old Mogadishu neighborhood. There was no one around; the only sounds were snipers shooting randomly. I crept into what was left of our house.

Home felt good even with the roof, doors, and windows gone. Everything else had been looted. I found a shovel, went into my old bedroom, and dug a hole six feet deep that I could jump in at night when the shelling started. In there every night, like a grave, I hummed songs and closed my eyes to make myself forget about the whistling rockets and thudding explosions. I was always surprised to wake up in the morning alive. Outside, every morning, was more destruction and dead bodies. But those like me who stayed behind also came out, chatted, and prayed together. I walked around the neighborhood, checking on people. All the faces I knew were gone. Falis was gone. Faisa and her family had left for Ethiopia; we never said goodbye. Would I ever see her again?

In the city, I came out to the KM4 circle and saw that a few businesses had reopened. Next to the Fathi restaurant was a phone store called Al-Imra Electronic. I went in and asked for a cheap phone with a memory chip. For thirty-five dollars, it came with a SIM card service that could let me send emails. I sent my first that night to Paul, giving him my phone number. It had been a month since we met. He called me an hour later. We talked until the shelling started and I had to jump into my hole. "I have to go, Paul. Bye!"

Then I figured out how I could download songs to my little phone—Jennifer Lopez, Ja Rule, Michael Jackson, and 50 Cent—and listen while hunkered down in my hole.

The music helped me fall asleep. In the morning, I left the memory chip with all the songs in the hole, buried under the earth. If al-Shabaab caught me with that, I would surely be killed.

A few NGOs—nongovernmental organizations, or nonprofit groups—had started operating at the government bases in Mogadishu, with funds from UN agencies based in Kenya. Because of this, more Somalis became interested in learning English so they could work with the aid staff. One day I got called to teach English at a house in the neighborhood, to a Somali woman and her kids. I taught her basic lessons on how to communicate with foreigners. On a small blackboard with white chalk, I wrote down English sentences and vocabulary.

Once I made some money from tutoring, I decided it might be safe enough to renew my old English classes—this time along KM4 Street, which was now filled with other businesses. I found an empty shop space and moved in. I made a chalkboard from a piece of wood that had been painted black, and bought some chalk. I wrote the first lesson on the board, hoping some students would show up. To be safe, I decided the instruction should focus on the Koran in English. That way, no one could say I was being anti-Islamist.

After a few days, some students started showing up. They liked the lessons about Islam, so I put together more. It was exciting to see them thrive in the classroom, getting excited about new words and ways to communicate. But when one of my students, a teenager, died in a nearby explosion, I decided it was too dangerous to hold school in a public place. Instead, I went back to my earlier method, going from house to house, teaching people who lived in the government area and who could afford to pay me. I was even starting to save some money.

But in Mogadishu, your presence never goes unnoticed. One morning my phone rang. The caller ID displayed, "NO NUMBER." I answered. "Hello?"

"Is this the one they call Abdi American?" said a man's voice.

"Yes," I said, thinking it must be someone I knew. "Who is this?"

"You must drop that wicked nickname. We know who you are; we know where you live."

"Sorry. Okay. But that's not my nickname anymore. It is an old name."

"You are lucky I called. I have warned you." And then he hung up.

• 12 •

MESSAGES FROM MOGADISHU

By 2008, Somalia had been at war for seventeen years, but calling this living hell a "war" was too polite. It was really just endless gory terrorism against starving civilians who didn't even care anymore which side won. A million people had been killed, and a million and a half forced from their homes. Half a million had now evacuated the city for the camp in Eelasha, where my mom and sister now lived. But some remained, like me, and some form of life was still going on inside the city despite the constant slaughter. There were cybercafés, shops, restaurants, and even colleges. I paid five dollars and enrolled in the Somali Institute of Management and Administration, which promised to teach math, English, computer programs, Arabic, Sharia law, Tarbiyah (Islamic moral education), administration, and management. I was asked to take an English placement test and answered all the questions. I started in a class with twenty-five students, learning English and computer. Our teacher, Mr. Wewe, was surprised at how well I answered the English questions. Other students asked me how I learned this English. I couldn't say I learned from movies because someone in the class could be al-Shabaab, so I said I learned it from reading the class books.

Classes were always fun, but getting to school was not. One day I was in a bus behind another bus that drove over a roadside bomb, killing most of the passengers, some of them students I knew well. Another day a rocket hit the college itself, killing students and teachers. None of this closed the school or stopped us from going.

After classes one afternoon in early 2009, I went into a cybercafé and saw an email from Paul.

> Keep your head down, Abdi. [Somalia] is getting
> a lot of international news. By the way, how old
> are you now? I'd like to write a short piece about
> how you and others who have been sending news
> emails—I won't use your full name, if that is a
> security problem, but I would like readers to know
> your age. And are you still teaching?

Not long after that, Paul wrote again with a link to his story in *The Atlantic*. It was titled "The War Is Bitter and Nasty," which was a quote from one of the emails I had sent him. A week or so later, around five o'clock, just before sunset, I was walking home when my phone rang with a strange number. I answered even though I was shaking, thinking it was al-Shabaab again.

"Hi, is this Abdi?"

It was a woman's voice, in American English. She sounded like a movie actress.

My heart was still pounding, but now from excitement. *Maybe this is someone from the U.S. government who wants to get me out of Somalia!*

"Yes, this is Abdi." The woman on the phone said she was Cori Princell, a producer for an American public radio show called *The Story*, which was hosted by Dick Gordon. They hired local people on the ground in places around the world and had them talk about their lives for American listeners. She had read Paul's article in *The Atlantic* and wanted to discuss a diary recording project with me.

We spoke for twenty minutes, until my battery died. I told her my frustration in the city, how I wanted to live a life like everyone else in the world. How I was trying to make something out of my life by going to college.

"I don't have a future here," I said. "I could die any time . . . who knows? Everything I enjoy has been taken from me. I live in a world isolated from the rest of the world. I dream of going to America. I know I belong in that country."

Just before my battery died, she said, "Abdi, we would love to share your voice with our listeners. Please let me know, and stay safe."

I thought about her offer. Part of me said no. *What if al-Shabaab is listening to American radio or reading the website?*

They know me: I'm the one they call American. The other part of me said I would be crazy not to try. I wanted to break the barrier around me and connect myself to the world. I wanted to tell my story. *This is finally my chance to be who I want to be!* I thought. *My voice will be known in America, like the Hollywood stars!*

I emailed Hassan. He wrote back:

> Do it. Do it. This is a chance. Don't waste it. Al-Shabaab don't read the website of *The Story.* Your audience will be in America not in Somalia. This is not the BBC. So say yes.

So I said yes. I did not tell my mom, who would have had a heart attack. America had sponsored the Ethiopian troops in Somalia and led air strikes that took many lives. America was fighting Islam across the Middle East. America by now was the most hated country in Somalia.

In the black stillness of a November night in 2009, I crawled six feet under the ground in my bedroom hidey-hole, pushed the "record" button on my cell phone, and started speaking to America.

> *It is midnight. Pitch-dark. I can hear gunshots ringing. Heavy shelling landing. This might be my last night on earth. Or I might survive.*

I talked about my mom, my sister, Faisa, and the movies—all the good things that happened before.

I am a schoolteacher in the most dangerous city,
Mogadishu. Before things got as bad as they are
now, we at least had something to entertain us.
Every night we would go to cinemas and come
home late at night. I used to watch American
Hollywood films. I couldn't miss one. I was a
movie buff. Most of my friends and my girlfriend
would call me the American. It's a name they gave
me after seeing how I speak American English. I
always like to keep my hair long and styled, and I
always like to dress in an elegant way. And I have
taught myself to walk, pump iron, and speak En-
glish like the carefree stars I have watched more
often in Hollywood movies.

Every night I would record a diary. At the cybercafé, I visited the website of *The Story* and heard my reports. My stories were titled "Messages from Mogadishu" and were introduced by Dick Gordon, the show's host. He called me "our reporter" and "our man in Mogadishu." It made me feel official.

After I filed a report called "Surviving Mogadishu," emails flooded into *The Story*. One came from a doctor at Dartmouth College named Sharon McDonnell, who said she was extremely moved by my recordings. The email carried the subject line "Gorgeous, Exquisite and Painful." She wrote,

I worked in Afghanistan and various parts of
Africa and the Middle East. Every element of the

story was brought to life by Dick Gordon and the understated way that Abdi tells his story.

I wrote back,

> Hi Sharon,
> This is Abdi from Mogadishu. I got a forward of your email to *The Story with Dick Gordon.* I wanted to thank you for your kind feeling and appreciation. Mogadishu had been this way and worse for twenty years, without central government. I had never seen peace for my life. I had been experiencing the worst through my life. Al-Shabaab and the government are fighting for the third day of constant firing and shelling. I didn't go out to my teaching these three days. I earn living by teaching English. I would like to flee but there is no way I can do that with no money. My mom is in the camps.

And then came an email from Sharon, who said she was the mom of a son and wanted to help me: "Is there any way I can help?"

I felt my American dream was cracking open slowly. Every email from Sharon after that was full of hope. She introduced me to winter, attaching photos of her house in Maine with snow covering the ground. She sent a picture of her family. Then we started speaking on the phone. Sharon was asking about ways I could leave. But where to go? She wanted to send me some money, so I told her how to do it safely. *The Story* was also sending me payments for my reports. Five hundred dollars from *The Story*, $300 from Sharon, $200, $100. One day I handed my mom $150. She had her mouth wide open and did not believe it.

"How did you get this much money?" she asked.

It was time to break the secret to her. I told her about the radio work, meeting Sharon, everything. I told her that some good human beings, Americans, non-Muslim, sent all this money not only to me but to my family.

"Mom, eat well," I told her. "That's all your money."

I let her know that through this generosity, Hassan also had enough money to survive and pay rent. Mom was able to hire three men to build a nice hut that could fit her, Nima, and my niece. Thick enough to protect them from the sun and the dust, and to cook out of the wind. They could buy food and water.

Back in the city, I kept going to college, with dollars hidden in my clothes. I communicated with Sharon every day. When our Internet was down, Hassan would email her on my behalf. The discussions about leaving Somalia continued; Kenya seemed the best option. But leaving my mom behind was my biggest worry. If something happened to her, if she got injured, I would want to be there to help. Then I thought, *If I stay here, I will surely die and she will have no help anyway.*

Sharon organized a group she called Team Abdi. It included Ben Bellows, an American former student of hers working as a doctor in Kenya, Cori Princell and Dick Gordon from *The Story*, the journalist Paul Salopek, Hassan, and Sharon's family. Their mission was to get me out of Somalia. Plan A was getting me a visa to Kenya. But the immigration official in Nairobi just laughed when Ben asked for one. He said they don't grant visas to Somalis, ever. Somalis in Kenya are classified as refugees and are not allowed to work. They are supposed to be confined to those desperate refugee camps near the border. Yet hundreds of thousands of Somalis lived in Nairobi; they owned shops, restaurants, and services. Somalis bought food and clothes and paid rent. They were responsible for roughly a third of all economic activity in the city. Still, the Kenyan authorities pretended they did not exist, perhaps out of fear that acknowledging them would encourage more migration. So Somalis were forced to avoid the police and survive by their wits. So much for Plan A.

Plan B was an overland trip using smugglers, as Hassan had done years earlier. But that had become impossibly dangerous under al-Shabaab. You would be killed at the first roadblock.

More than a year passed as I continued to file reports for *The Story*. We kept discussing safe ways to get me out. Then, on a Saturday evening in March 2011, my house was bombed when I was out. I returned to see that there was nothing left but rubble. That night I slept at the corner of the street, in a dusty space behind a neem tree. When I woke up in the morning, I learned that Team Abdi had put together five hundred dollars to buy me a plane ticket out of Somalia. I immediately got a passport with more money I'd saved up. But where was I going? What country would give me an entry visa?

While I was getting my passport, Team Abdi learned that I could fly directly from Mogadishu to Kampala, Uganda, and get a one-day Ugandan visa upon landing. That would give me twenty-four hours to find a way from Kampala into neighboring Kenya, to meet up with my brother. I went to the airline agency, showed my passport, and bought a ticket to Kampala.

My flight was in three days. The safe thing would have been to lie low in Mogadishu until then, but I could not leave without saying goodbye to my mom. So, the day before my flight, I stashed my plane ticket and phone under the debris of our house and made the dangerous minibus journey one last time to the miserable Eelasha camp. Inside, I was trembling that someone would recognize me as the recruit who had deserted after just one day.

Mom was cooking over a fire outside her new hut when I arrived. I whispered to her that I was leaving the next day on an airplane, and she stopped stirring her pot. She could think of nothing to say. Finally she told me she was happy and that this was a good thing. I said goodbye to Nima and told them both not to tell anyone of my plans.

"Wherever we end up, I'll see you when I see you," I said. Then I shook hands with my mom; under al-Shabaab it was forbidden even for a mom and grown son to hug, and there was no point in risking attention.

That night, after I returned to Mogadishu, I slept for the last time in my hidey-hole, which I had cleared of enough debris in order to crawl in.

To my surprise, the next morning my mom showed up. She had taken a bus from the camp.

"Mom, why are you here?" I was worried her presence would attract attention.

"I wanted to say goodbye to you," she said.

We walked together to the airport. I had no bag, no extra clothes, nothing that would look like I was going on a journey—just a guy taking a walk. Carefully hidden in my clothes were my plane ticket, my passport, my freshly charged phone, and seventy dollars.

The airport terminal entrance was guarded by Ugandan troops from the African Union mission. A soldier barked at us: "Only passengers allowed!"

I fished out my ticket. He inspected it warily.

"You may enter," he said. "Not her."

I turned to Mom. "So this is finally goodbye," I said.

"Goodbye, my son. I am so happy for you, and I will pray for you."

It was all I could do not to cry in front of that soldier. I felt so sad, but my mom's blessing helped.

The plane's engines were running; it was ready for a takeoff. There were not many people on the flight. I took a window seat, my phone ringing with calls from Paul, Cori, and Sharon. "I am on the plane," I told them. "I will check with you when we land." As the plane backed away from the terminal, I looked out and saw my mom standing there in the sun, waiting for us to take off. She passed from my view. I could no longer hold back my tears. I wept in silence for a long time. Then I saw other passengers were crying too.

When the plane lifted off, everyone prayed to Allah for a safe flight. The plane climbed so fast I was surprised how quickly we were high above the city. The hot sun was glinting sharply off the tin roofs of the buildings of Mogadishu. I felt like I had broken out of a prison. My future was a mystery, but at least I was leaving hell forever.

After a brief stop in Nairobi, we were on our way to Kampala. Upon arrival, all the Somalis on the flight were directed to go into one of the waiting halls. There were no seats. Pregnant women, crying children, elderly people who seemed sick and weak—we all sat on the hard airport floor. My phone had no service. I paced back and forth, wondering what was happening.

Hours passed. No one came. Other passengers, wearing nice clothes and transiting to other countries in Europe and North America, walked past us. None of us cared. At least we were lying on a floor made of tiles, not a dusty road with dogs and graves. I was so tired I fell asleep on the floor with a bunch of other Somalis. It was past midnight when an officer with a cell phone in his hand stood above us and spoke. I was only half-awake and thought I was dreaming when he said, "Who is Abdi Iftin?"

Everyone woke up.

"Excuse me," I said. "I am Abdi Iftin." I followed him into a tiny room. Without saying anything, he handed me a phone.

"Hey, Abdi. How are you?"

It was Ben Bellows in Nairobi. He had called the airport to assure the authorities that I had a place to stay for the night and that I had a bus ticket for Kenya in the morning. Ben said Team Abdi had made me a reservation to spend the night at a Kampala hotel, and my bus ticket to Nairobi was waiting for me there. Someone from the hotel had been waiting for hours outside the airport, holding a sign with my name on it. She had finally left, said Ben.

At one in the morning, my passport stamped for a twenty-four-hour visit, I walked out of the airport into the dark night. I shivered in the strange cold, something I had never felt. Immediately, I was surrounded by a scrum of taxi drivers shouting at me in Swahili and English. I was so cold and hungry I just felt frozen in place. Then came another piece of good luck. At that moment, a middle-aged man shoved his way through the crowd of drivers and spoke to me in Somali. He was a taxi driver and warned me that the others were trying to overcharge me.

We got in his car and he pushed a cassette tape into the player—Somali music! I had not heard it in so long. He told me his name was Aleey and he had left Somalia ten years earlier. He had crossed into Kenya, then moved to Kampala, where life was more hospitable for Somalis, though that was changing with the recent al-Shabaab attacks.

"Are you hungry?" he asked.

"Yes!"

"Let's eat here."

He pulled over at a small late-night kiosk and ordered a

soda and a *mandazi*, the delicious Kenyan version of dough-nuts. I ordered the same thing. Then he brought me to buy a SIM card.

"Where are you staying?" he asked.

"It's called the Shalom Guest House."

"Oh! What? No, no, that is not possible! What do you do, my friend?" He seemed surprised, as if he'd been expect-ing me to stay elsewhere. He explained that he had driven many rich white people to this hotel but never a Somali. Then again, he had never heard a Somali speak English like me. He felt sure I must have just flown in from London, and he refused to believe my story. I understood. I could hardly believe it myself.

On the way to the hotel, I called Hassan, then Ben, Sharon, Cori, Paul, and Dick. Everyone was so relieved that I had made it safely to Uganda. Aleey dropped me at the Guest House, and we exchanged phone numbers. He waved goodbye. "I will come for you tomorrow to show you around town," he said.

I walked up to the receptionist, who handed me the key to my room. She said they had been expecting me much earlier. She knew nothing about my struggles. My room had big glass windows and a huge TV screen. There was a freshly made king-size bed, bigger than my mom's entire hut in the camp. And a shower. On a desk was a sealed envelope with my name on it. Inside was a bus ticket to Nairobi and three hundred dollars in cash. Ben had a friend in Kampala who had dropped it at the hotel.

I was so tired, but I felt I needed to get clean before

I could sleep. I stood there in the shower wondering why there was no bucket, and what all the knobs did. I turned one and was surprised when water dropped from a nozzle like a stream, cold and scary. I went down to ask the receptionist for a bucket. She laughed. "You don't need a bucket," she said. "I will show you."

Back in the room, the lady showed me how to work the knobs and make the water come out nice and warm. Hot water without starting a fire! I felt stupid but I thanked her and she left. Then I stood under that water and turned the knob until it was steaming hot. I stood there for a long time, in a trance, washing away the dirt and blood and pain of Mogadishu. I stood there until all that hot water was gone.

• 13 •

LITTLE MOGADISHU

I woke up late with the TV remote still in my hand. I must have fallen asleep watching movies. There were many missed calls on my phone from Team Abdi. Time was running short. I had to leave Uganda that night for Kenya to meet up with Hassan.

I called Aleey, the taxi driver. He said he was already waiting for me at the hotel reception. I threw on my clothes—no bag to pack—and went downstairs. There were several white people getting ready for their day of tourism in Uganda. They had fancy backpacks, and they were stuffing them with hats, sunscreen, lunches, and water bottles. I got into Aleey's taxi, and I told him to take me to the bus station. He looked at me like I was crazy.

"Don't take the bus!" he said. "It's a trap! They will find you at the border and send you back to Uganda, and then

Uganda will put you on a flight to Mogadishu. They have done this to so many people I know."

By now I felt I could trust Aleey, but I said I had no other options.

"I know a better way," he said. "You can catch a ride on a tanker truck to the border. There, after nightfall, you can take a *boda-boda* across the bush into Kenya and meet the truckers on the other side."

A *boda-boda* was a motorcycle taxi. Aleey told me that along the Uganda-Kenya border, young men earned money by smuggling Somalis into Kenya on their motorcycles, avoiding the road crossings.

"It's the best way," said Aleey. I called Hassan to ask what he thought.

"I think he's right," agreed my brother. "If they check for visas on the bus, you will not be allowed into Kenya."

We drove back to Kisenyi, Kampala's Somali neighborhood, and parked at a gas station where a tanker truck was filling up. Aleey spoke to two Ugandan drivers who were drinking tea. They approached me and said it would cost one hundred dollars for the ride. I handed them the cash. I said goodbye to my new friend, Aleey, wondering if I would ever see him again.

"Hide here," one of the men said in English, pointing to the tiny sleeper bunk behind the seats. "Don't make any move. Stay still."

"Don't worry, my friend," said the other as I climbed in. "You will be in Kenya soon."

We lurched off down the road.

The road was bad and I kept banging around in that bunk. Hours passed, and we were still in Uganda. The two men played rap music all the way. Finally, at four o'clock in the morning, we were a few miles from the border. The tanker truck pulled slowly into a side street, parked, and opened the doors.

"Come. Come. Come," one whispered to me. "Go there, catch a *boda-boda*."

I hopped out of the truck and ran across the street into a dark narrow alley. I could not see anything except the dim light of a motorcycle.

"*Lete,*" the motorbike man said in Swahili. —Let's go.

"How much?"

"Ten dollars."

"No. Five dollars," I replied. I was getting better at bargaining for my various forms of transport.

"Okay. *Lete.*"

I climbed onto the bike behind him. We took off through the forest and in five minutes were over the border in Kenya. The truck was there waiting for me. It was still dark when we rolled into the town of Kisumu. It was still more than 150 miles to the city of Nairobi. We pulled into a parking lot; the drivers said they were too tired to go on. "Let's sleep here and proceed in the morning." They spread a piece of a cloth under the truck to sleep on. The night was dead quiet. The men quietly lit cigarettes. I quickly fell asleep. When the sun rose, I woke up under the truck to the sound of Kenyans coming to work. The place we had parked was an outdoor repair shop with many junk cars and components sitting everywhere. The two drivers were gone.

"Wewe amka!" A shirtless man was telling me to move on in Swahili. He needed to work on the truck and I was under it. I asked where the drivers were, but no one knew. I waited for an hour, two hours, three hours, but they never returned. I called Hassan; he was worried and so was everyone else on the team. By now it was obvious the drivers had betrayed me. I had paid them for a ride all the way to Nairobi, but I was hours away and on my own. I checked my pockets and was glad to find I still had money hidden in my pants. I was going to need it.

I walked around the muddy streets of town, past market stalls. Traders were selling hay, sugarcane, and pyramids of fruits. Women carried huge baskets on their heads. I did not know where to go. Then I heard a voice calling: "Nairobi, Nairobi, Nairobi!"

It was a minibus conductor shouting out to passengers. I hopped on. The bus, known as a *matatu*, was packed. The stereo was blasting Bob Marley, when the conductor in the front passenger seat stretched out his hand to collect the fare. "Five hundred shillings," he said in English.

I knew that was about five dollars. I had no Kenyan money, so I handed him my last twenty-dollar bill. He gave me back some change in Kenyan shillings but not nearly enough. When I argued with him in English, he replied angrily in a native dialect I couldn't understand, so I let it go.

"My friend, are you Somali?" asked a man sitting next to

me, in English. He was middle-aged and wore eyeglasses, and he smiled despite the discomfort of the journey.

"I am," I said.

"Oh, I love the Somali people! But I hate al-Shabaab. I have seen them on TV. Very bad."

We became instant friends, and he acted like a tour guide. I kept asking him the names of towns we were passing. Everything was very green like I had never seen; corn and hay grew everywhere. The road to Nairobi was so clean and smooth. Fancy cars sped past us. We stopped at a police checkpoint and my heart was beating fast, but the officer said something to the conductor and waved us on. It was not Mogadishu; they didn't care where women sat or if we had beards. The afternoon turned to dusk, and soon the setting sun reflected off the skyscrapers of downtown Nairobi. It was so beautiful! The streetlights were switching on everywhere. I had never seen so many lights. I felt like a caveman dropped into the modern world. People outside were standing in groups talking, laughing, enjoying the evening. I texted Hassan, my heart pounding with excitement. Our bus inched through traffic, passing market stalls, banks, government buildings, and churches. Everything was a wonder to me. Finally, we pulled into the chaotic Accra Road *matatu* station, and I descended in a daze.

The station was so busy, people shouting and bumping into each other. It was like watching bees. Then someone tapped my shoulder.

"Abdi!" he said in a deep voice I did not recognize. I turned and felt I was looking into a mirror. It was my brother, Hassan, but in adulthood he had become just like me—tall, thin, the same long face and wide brow. *When did we become twins?* We hugged and held each other for several minutes. Both our phones were ringing from Team Abdi trying to find out if we had met, but we ignored them and just hugged.

After getting food, we jumped into a *matatu* headed for Eastleigh, the neighborhood also known as Little Mogadishu. We arrived around nine at night, but the place was as bright and busy as day. Every stall, every kiosk, and every shop was run by Somalis. Somali music and American rap were blasting from everywhere. The streets were filthy like Mogadishu. I didn't care. I just stood there and marveled at all the stuff for sale—shoes, clothes, belts, milk, candy, chewing gum, soccer balls. Anything you wanted. I smelled fried samosas and saw steam rising from teapots. Restaurants were selling goat, camel, and cow meat with rice. It was like being in Mogadishu but with no bombs.

My joy was interrupted by a sudden clamor from the crowd, followed by panic and running in all directions, like frightened cattle. I had not heard any explosion, so I couldn't understand why all the Somalis were running. Hassan grabbed me by the hand.

"This way!" he yelled. We turned down an alley, and ran.

"What is going on?" I asked, panting.

"The police," said my brother. "They come like this every night to rob the Somalis."

After a few minutes the police were gone and everyone was back on the street, business as usual. Tea shops filled up, and conversations went on, just like nothing happened. I was starting to think maybe life in Nairobi was no paradise.

Hassan had reserved a room for both of us at the Hotel Medina for one night. This was one of the best hotels in Eastleigh, with running water and a restaurant, owned by Somalis, but he chose it because it had the same name as our mom. We went to our room and I told Hassan about my adventures. He told me about his own long journey to Nairobi, which he had only hinted at in his emails. We talked until three o'clock in the morning, when we both fell asleep.

At sunrise, I awoke to the cries of the conductors calling out the destinations of their *matatus*. Eastleigh in the morning was a noisy place. I looked out the window. Young Somali men, dressed and shaved like American gangster rappers, wearing headphones, walked along jamming to music. Beautiful Somali women in colorful dresses, and Kenyan women of the Kikuyu tribe. Music was everywhere, people laughing and dancing. This place was lit!

We checked out of the hotel. Hassan and I had a list of things to do on that Sunday; first was buying me some new clothes and a haircut, then visiting Ben Bellows. I bought a pair of jeans for five dollars, and a T-shirt with the American flag for three dollars. Then I walked into a Somali barbershop. There were portraits of soccer players, rappers, and actors all over the walls. When it was my turn, I pointed to Usher, the American singer. "Like that," I said. Sides trimmed down to skin, top and back growing wild. So cool.

Next I bought a necklace, a wristband, and some sneakers. I was sure no one looked more American than me. Hassan laughed. I changed so much in one day, but freedom from al-Shabaab felt like the best gift in the entire world.

Later on, we jumped onto a *matatu* and headed to a nice restaurant across town to meet Ben Bellows and his wife, Nicole. They were so happy to see me and glad that they had helped me reunite with Hassan. The menu was confusing. We didn't know what to choose, but burgers seemed like the most American dish, so we both ordered one. After the meal, we visited Ben and Nicole's house. Before we went back to Hassan's room, they handed us money to help with getting me settled.

The building where Hassan lived was home to dozens of Somalis, each family squeezing into one tiny room. The stairs, pitch-black even by day, creaked and swayed so much I felt they would collapse any time. People washed clothes in buckets and hung them on their balconies, dripping down on the street below. Cockroaches crawled on the walls. Of course this is the way tens of millions of Africans live, in cities across the continent, so residents of Little Mogadishu were just grateful to be out of a war zone.

Hassan lived on the third floor. The room was small but at least had windows facing the street. There was no furniture, no bathroom, no kitchen. Rolled up in the corner was a single foam mattress and a pillow; we used some of the money from Ben and Nicole to buy another set for me. None of this mattered or bothered me once I saw the main attraction in his room: a Toshiba laptop and piles of DVDs of Hollywood movies. Hassan told me there were thousands of DVDs sold on the streets of Nairobi. I was thrilled. Besides my night in the hotel in Uganda, I hadn't watched movies since Faisa's shack had been shut down.

That Monday morning, after bread and tea, we jumped into a *matatu* to the office of the United Nations High Commissioner for Refugees (UNHCR). Because I had been smuggled into Kenya, I was not yet registered as a refugee, which was the first step in getting to the United States. I was carrying all the letters sent by Team Abdi. The line stretched around the building. After four hours we finally got inside, and I was seated with a hundred other people in a waiting room. Six hours later, a Kenyan man in a dark suit came out.

"Time out today!" he yelled. "Come back tomorrow."

My heart sank. We'd just have to get there early the next day. There was the same long line in the chilly morning, though. Day after day, we were rejected from even meeting with someone.

Finally, we approached one of the security guards, and Hassan spoke to him in Swahili: "I will pay you."

The guard took Hassan to a place where the security camera could not catch him, and we handed him two thousand shillings—about twenty dollars. He let me into the waiting room. At three o'clock in the afternoon, another man called my name. He took my picture and fingerprints, then led me to a desk for the paperwork. I was officially registered as a refugee living in Kenya! Now I could begin to seek refugee protection and resettlement in the West.

Every day after that, Hassan and I went to the UNHCR, hoping for a protection interview. Since coming to Nairobi,

Hassan had been interviewed more than ten times. On the wall of the building, they posted names of people selected for protection and resettlement. Hassan had been checking the list for years. He was never picked. But now, with all the letters of support from our American friends, we thought our chances were high. Still it was always the same: the officials wrote down our phone numbers but never called for an interview. We saw other Somalis whose names were posted, tears of relief running down their faces. It was hard to watch; we could not share their joy. Real life only began for those who were selected.

I continued to file radio reports for *The Story,* now from the BBC studio in downtown Nairobi. Instead of life in a war zone, I told Americans about life as a refugee in Little Mogadishu. One big difference between Little Mogadishu and real Mogadishu: in the Nairobi version, you didn't wake up every morning wondering if this would be your last day on earth. So that was a definite plus. But Little Mogadishu was still a daily test. You were on your own, and survival depended on your strength, wits, and good luck. The Kenyan government and the UNHCR offered no help to the hundreds of thousands of Somali refugees living there; it was like we didn't exist. Everyone had to fetch food, clothing, and shelter for himself, but refugee documents were not work permits, so there was no official way to earn money for those things. Your documents did not protect you from police harassment either. When I would eventually come to the United States, I would see how Mexican, Central American, and South American immigrants faced similar issues there.

You felt trapped in Little Mogadishu. To the west, between Little Mogadishu and the skyscrapers of downtown, is the feared Pangani police station, from which corrupt officers fan out every night in search of bribes from refugees. To the north is the vast and notorious Mathare slum, one of the worst in all Africa. But within Little Mogadishu was an armed Somali youth gang who called themselves the Super Powers. Those gang members realized the Kenyan police did not care about protecting people in Little Mogadishu; refugees *ran* from the police, so they could never dare to report a crime. The gang members took advantage of that, terrorizing residents, snatching cell phones and cash at gunpoint, knowing they could get away with it. One night, two Super Power guys held Hassan by the neck right in front of our building. They took his phone and some cash, then let him go. Another night, they chased me down an alley, but I managed to outrun them.

Fortunately, there were a lot of places to blend in with the crowd. On just about every street, you will find a mosque, a *hawala* (a money-wiring shop), a small shopping mall, tea shops, photo studios, barbershops, and tall apartment complexes crammed with people. Even Kenyans do their weekly food shopping in Little Mogadishu.

Meanwhile, Hassan and I kept trying to get resettlement interviews, with no luck. Sharon called from Maine. A friend of hers, a teacher at the University of Massachusetts, named Margaret Caudill, was leading a group of American nursing students to Kenya to improve cardiovascular and metabolic health in rural areas. The project was called Afya

Njema, "Good Health." Hassan and I were invited to volunteer for them. With nothing else to do and tired of waiting for something to change, we gladly accepted. I was assigned to register the patients, then measure their weights and heights. Hassan, who by now spoke fluent Swahili, had to translate for the elderly Kenyans who didn't speak English.

Margaret had brought some cash from Sharon for Hassan and me. It was enough for us to set up a street business selling socks and shoes, so we started doing that. We worked seventeen hours a day to make enough to buy food and pay rent, waking up at five in the morning to grab the best spot on the side of the road and not going home until midnight. But it felt good to pay our own way and not constantly need money from Sharon.

After weeks of hard work and with a little cash in my pocket, I went to hang out at the Balanbaalis Studio, a social club where young Somalis would dress up, dance to loud American music, and drink Cokes. There I ran into a well-dressed young woman named Muna. She was short, and not as skinny as most Somalis, probably because she had grown up in Little Mogadishu, not starving. She was living with some roommates and was very independent. New refugees could tell she knew so much more about the world than they did. Watching her walk down First Avenue was like watching a confident American woman on the streets of New York. She feared nothing and was not the least bit shy like most Somali girls. People looked up to her, especially the neighborhood men, whom she completely ignored. Muna was mad about America and determined to marry a man who could bring her there. Naturally, I felt we had much in common, and I decided to pursue her.

When I told her I was interested in dating her, she laughed. "You have no money. Why would I date you?"

"Because they call me Abdi American," I said. I knew this was a thin argument, but it was my only card to play.

She stared at me, taking in my accent. "Are you from Mogadishu?"

"Yes."

"What's it like?"

"You have never been?"

"No," she said. "My family was displaced from the south. I grew up in the camps."

Eventually, she got right to the point: "Abdi, you are wasting your time, bro. I am not going to date a man in Little Mogadishu. How can I date someone who is broke like me?"

Still, it was nice to sit with her. Later, I came up with an idea. I went to the Obama Photography Studio and had them Photoshop my picture standing next to the Empire State Building, the White House, and other famous places in the United States. I went on Facebook and updated my residence to California. I posted all the photos. When Muna saw it, she said she broke out laughing. It was worth it for that.

...

Al-Shabaab already had a presence in the refugee camps in northeast Kenya, and they were getting more aggressive in the country. In October 2011 they kidnapped two Spanish aid workers from Doctors Without Borders, taking them into Somalia as hostages. In response the Kenyan government declared war on al-Shabaab. They sent troops, tanks, helicopters, and artillery to battle the terrorists deep inside Somalia.

It was called Operation Linda Nchi, "To Protect the Nation," but the residents of Little Mogadishu had a pretty good idea we were not going to be protected. As the troops marched across the Somali border, police encircled Little Mogadishu, assuming that residents there would heed the call of al-Shabaab to retaliate against Kenya. Soon the streets were cleared, and businesses were closed. Everyone went home and turned on the TV. Hassan and I locked our door and sat quietly. Outside we heard sporadic shots.

Life changed overnight in Little Mogadishu. Police night raids increased, especially in mosques. Men with beards were taken out. Executive orders were announced: all refugees must leave Nairobi and go to the camps. This was the beginning of the hide-and-seek games between us and the police.

Soon after that, Hassan and I were on our way out of our apartment, when two men in civilian clothes walked up quickly behind us.

"Show me your IDs or passports, please," one of them said.

We stopped and looked at them. They brought out handcuffs.

"Where are your Kenyan IDs or passports?"

"We don't have Kenyan IDs," Hassan said. "We have refugee documents."

As I reached into my pocket for my refugee document, the man handcuffed me and told me to follow him.

"Where are you taking me?" I asked. "Please show me your police ID."

From his leather jacket he pulled out an ID; I couldn't tell if it was real or fake. I tried to protest the arrest, and he pulled out a gun. He led me to a corner of the street where fewer people walked. Hassan was brought by the other man.

"I will take you to the Pangani station!" the man holding me shouted. My heart froze, but then the negotiation started. "How much do you have?" he asked. "Give me a thousand shillings!"

"I don't have it," I said.

"Seven hundred!"

"I only have one hundred."

He pulled my wallet out of my pocket, shuffled through it, and took the hundred-shilling note. He smiled, tucked away his pistol, and left, no doubt to find another refugee he could mug. Hassan also negotiated his way out of the other man's threat. We walked away realizing how vulnerable we, as refugees, were to this kind of thievery. Kenyans didn't seem to care about what happened to the people in Little Mogadishu, as if our lives were less valuable. And who could we report crimes to when it was the police who were committing them? The dim light at the end of our dark tunnel was the hope that someday our American friends might help us escape.

The police raids in Little Mogadishu and the Kenyan troops in Somalia were all good news to al-Shabaab; it was exactly the chaos they craved. They soon escalated the fight, throwing hand grenades and bombs in public spaces. The Kenyans blamed *all* Somalis, not just the ones committing acts of violence. "Get Them Out of Our Country!" the newspaper headlines shouted.

After several unexploded bombs were retrieved from an apartment in Little Mogadishu, more young men in the neighborhood were dragged off to jail. Often they never returned. There was no way to identify terrorists—they had the same refugee papers we did—so any young man was treated as a suspect. Hassan and I kept our heads down, with our hearts in our throats. When Hassan and I had to be separated, we would text each other, making sure we were okay. Women were no safer; the police were raping them. All of the people who lived in our building exchanged phone numbers. When the police were coming, we would all text each other: "They are coming down 6th street, run toward 5th." They would lock down their stores, hide in the bathrooms, under the beds.

Meanwhile, the Kenyan citizens had stopped coming to shop in Little Mogadishu. The neighborhood was sealed off and surrounded by police checkpoints. The local media did not report what was happening in Little Mogadishu, but I did. Dick Gordon, the host of *The Story*, was growing more worried for our safety. He mentioned that his daughter Pamela was working for the Red Cross of Canada in Nairobi. She invited us for coffee on the rich side of town at a fancy shopping center called the Westgate Mall. Hassan and I managed to evade the police checks and get on a *matatu*. The mall was like something I had seen in movies of California or Florida: huge, clean, with gardens and moving stairs and shops full of people—white people, Kenyans, Asians. Everything was so expensive. We had a nice talk with Pam. She gave us her mobile number. "In case something happens to you, call me," she said.

Because we had no luck getting resettlement interviews, Team Abdi's next plan was to get us American student visas. To improve our chances, and get some college experience, Hassan and I began taking online English classes with an English professor at Lyndon State College in Vermont, named Nene Riley, who had heard my radio reports. She assigned us to read literature and write essays summarizing the main points of the pieces, our reaction to them, and how they applied to our own society. We even spoke with several students from Lyndon State College. My writing steadily improved.

Then, with Sharon's help, we applied to Southern Maine Community College as international exchange students. Sharon and her family sent a letter to the college confirming that she would support us financially and that they were our American family in Maine. Hassan and I had to take something called the Test of English as a Foreign Language (TOEFL), which took half a day. We both passed, and soon after that, DHL Nairobi shipped official acceptance letters from the school.

We were going to college in America! The next step was getting our student visas. This required interviews at the U.S. embassy in Nairobi. To support our requests, Team Abdi had gathered letters of recommendation from seven U.S. senators, including Bernie Sanders of Vermont. With everything ready, we paid our interview fees and waited for the appointments.

My interview was a week before Hassan's. That morning I woke up at five, so nervous, and got on a *matatu* before the police would start searching for refugees. I couldn't risk being late. The interview was at eight. I got there at six. After an intensive security screening, I proceeded inside the embassy and joined a waiting room of people who looked just as excited and nervous. As I sat there, I thought of my mom and my sister back in Mogadishu. If I got the visa and went to the United States, I would go to college, get a good job, and send them money every week. Life would be great for all of us.

"B-20, proceed to Window Eight."

That was me. B-20. I stood up and walked to Window Eight. The man behind the counter was a middle-aged, bald-headed white American.

"How are you today?" he asked.

"I am fine, sir. How about yourself?" I used my best American accent, trying not to faint from my nerves.

"Not bad. Have you ever traveled to the U.S.?"

"No."

"Have you ever traveled to any other country besides Kenya and Somalia?"

"No. But I passed through Uganda on my way to Kenya."

"What do you do now in Nairobi?"

"I am a refugee here, sir."

"Did you ever go to college in Nairobi?"

"No."

"And Somalia?"

"Yes, I went to a college in Mogadishu but it collapsed before I finished."

"What are those letters in your hand?"

"These are letters of support from senators and other supporters. Do you want to see them?"

"Sure."

He glanced quickly at the letters, looked up at me, and said, "I am sorry. You don't qualify for the visa this time. Good luck wherever you end up." Then he handed everything back to me.

I was frozen. I could not leave his window. He turned to his computer and started typing.

"Sir," I said with tears in my eyes. But he ignored me and called the next person, B-21.

I walked out of the embassy like my dad when he returned to Mogadishu, crippled and wobbling. Like his, my dream had been destroyed. I felt I did not belong to this world and that I must have been created to have a permanent broken heart. I was so shaky that I was afraid of getting hit by a car, so I had to sit down and breathe. I texted

Hassan. Soon everyone on Team Abdi was sending me condolences. Hassan got denied a week later.

We tried one more time, after Ben and Paul emailed people they knew who worked at the embassy. Again we were denied. One of the requirements of student visas is that you must have strong family ties in your home country so you aren't tempted to stay in the United States after school. Of course staying in the United States was absolutely our goal, and the embassy officers probably knew that.

We decided to try to go to school in Kenya. It wouldn't change our refugee status or help us get to America on student visas, but at least we would be improving our lives. And the police were less likely to harass a refugee with an official student ID. With the financial support of Sharon and her family, we had nothing to lose. Hassan got into Kenya Methodist University, me to Africa Nazarene University. So, without too much trouble, we were both official college students, with student IDs. Classes would start in April 2013.

Excited to share that good news, I walked down to our favorite tea shop on Sixth Street and met my new friends Yonis, Farah, and Zakariye. We were drinking tea and talking about the usual things—life, girls, and sports—when something caught my eye across the street. There, on the door of the Internet café, was a new sign: NOTICE: APPLY NOW FOR THE AMERICAN GREEN CARD LOTTERY.

The green card lottery? I had never heard of the green card lottery, but Yonis said it was a way to get a visa just by being lucky. You applied online and waited to see if you were picked. It was all about luck, not the people you knew or the skills you had. The Internet café owner was charging twenty cents to make the application, so he was encouraging people to try.

"Let's do it," I said.

"Oh, forget it," said Farah. "It's a waste of time."

"You never know," I said. "It's only twenty cents!"

I dragged my friends across the street, and we sat down and googled the lottery. It was officially called the Diversity Immigrant Visa Program and was meant to give people from poor countries a shot at U.S. immigration. Every October, some eight to fifteen million people around the world apply, and only fifty thousand get visas—a fraction of 1 percent. Nobody in the café knew any Somali who had ever won.

I am sure that if the application fee had been fifty cents, I would not have bothered. But for twenty cents, which we all assumed we were just throwing away, my friends and I took the chance and applied that day. So did Hassan. All we could do after that was wait seven months for the results in May.

...

The New Year arrived and Kenya was consumed by its upcoming presidential election. On March 4, 2013, the country voted for Uhuru Kenyatta, son of Jomo Kenyatta (the first president of Kenya). The son ran on a platform of national security, vowing to wipe out al-Shabaab. This, of course, meant there were even more al-Shabaab attacks in retaliation. Somalis anticipated more police raids in Little Mogadishu, and on election night, we all stayed locked behind our doors, praying there would be no bombs. For months after the election, tensions were high everywhere in the city.

School started in April. I would be studying journalism, and I was excited to be in classes every day. The hard part was getting there because the campus was fifteen miles away in the Ongata Rongai neighborhood, two *matatu* rides away. Anywhere along the route, you could be hit by a suicide terrorist or a roadside bomb or grabbed by the police; anything could happen. One day I was in a *matatu* coming home from an exam when the passengers, noticing I was Somali, got worried that I was al-Shabaab and carrying a bomb in my backpack. They started yelling at the driver.

"Why is he here?"

"Kick him out!"

The driver pulled over to the side of the road and ordered me off. Unfortunately, he had stopped right in front of the Pangani Police Station. Al-Shabaab had bombed that station a few weeks earlier, and security was very tight. If I got off the bus there, I would be arrested at best, and maybe shot on sight. I begged the driver as the passengers kept shouting, "Kick him out!"

"I am a student!" I cried. "I am not a terrorist!" Finally, I turned my backpack upside down and emptied out all my books, pencils, and pens onto the floor of the bus. I held up my student ID for everyone to see. This argument went on for five minutes until the driver sped off, then dropped me away from the police station. I stopped carrying a backpack and wore only a T-shirt in public so I could not be accused of concealing a bomb.

Finally, May came, time for the lottery winners to be announced. My friends had forgotten about it, but not me. I had been thinking about it every day, waiting for the moment. I texted my friends to meet one afternoon at the Internet café.

We had to wait for a computer terminal, it was so packed with people checking the results. They had been coming since the morning, Kenyans, Ethiopians, Somalis, all of them walking out glum-faced.

"See, this thing is fake," said Yonis.

When we got a computer, Farah went first. No luck. Zakariye. No. Yonis. Same. I went last. As I entered my application number and date of birth, I thought about all the good luck I had received in my life. There was the time my family escaped execution on our flight from Mogadishu when that fighter recognized my dad; the time I met Paul by chance that day in Mogadishu, setting me on a path as a radio correspondent; Sharon hearing me on the radio in Maine one evening; Aleey, the Somali cab driver in Kampala who rescued me from Entebbe Airport. So much good luck. I clicked "submit," on the luckiest day of my life.

• 14 •

LONG ODDS

I thought it was a mistake. Nobody wins the green card lottery. I reentered my information, twice. Both times it said the same thing: "You have been randomly selected . . ."

People in the café went crazy, slapping me on the back and cheering. The owner was so happy—now he could brag about having a lucky café. "You're an American now!" he shouted. "You're going to the land of opportunity! Remember us back here!"

It went on and on, the handshakes and congratulations. I was in a state of bliss. When things calmed down, I finally had the chance to read further. The website did indeed say, "You have been randomly selected . . . ," but that wasn't the whole sentence. The rest of it said, "for further processing."

You have been randomly selected for further processing.

What did that mean? I read on. It turns out that winning

the green card lottery does not actually win you a green card. It wins you the chance to *apply* for a green card. Not everyone who applies will actually get a green card, so the lottery draws three times as many "winners" as there are actual green cards to give out. In 2013, I was one of 155,000 people chosen around the world to apply for just 55,000 green cards to be issued in 2014. About one chance in three.

That didn't seem too bad. I had beaten much worse odds in my life. But that wasn't all. The lottery winners are numbered, and the people with the smallest numbers get the first crack at applying for a green card. When some of those early winners fail to pass for whatever reason, the next numbers in line are invited to apply. When all the green cards are issued, the process ends for that year. If your number has not been called, it's all over. You lose your chance. And even if your number finally gets called, the cut-off date for diversity green cards is September 30 of the issuing year—2014 in my case. No more green cards would be issued after that date, regardless of whether all 55,000 had been awarded yet. The clock was ticking for everyone.

The first name chosen from the Africa region received case number 2014AF00000001. Number one. My case number was 2014AF00047441. I had to read it carefully several times to figure out it meant there were more than 47,000 people ahead of me. In Africa. Not counting other winners all over the world, trying for the same visas. It seemed like impossible odds. For me to get to America, I had to hope tens of thousands of other desperate people around the world lost out. That didn't feel right.

The math was bad, but the paperwork seemed even more daunting. If I ever did get an interview to apply for a visa, I would need all sorts of documentation about who I was, and what I've been doing all my life. But the U.S. government didn't recognize any civil documents from Somalia—no Somali passports, birth certificates, divorce papers, or marriage licenses were accepted. In other words, I needed to produce civil records to escape a country that was so broken that we had no civil records.

The one hope was that Somalis could sometimes get a waiver on those documents. But other paperwork was always required, starting with a medical certificate to determine that I was healthy. I didn't think that would be too hard, but I'd never been to a doctor in my life, so I really didn't know. Then you had to get school transcripts, but with all the police raids, I could not get to school every day. My attendance was poor despite my best efforts. The worst requirement, the one that filled me with dread, was obtaining something called a Letter of Good Conduct, certifying I was not a criminal. Of course I was no criminal and had no record, but getting proof of that required walking into Nairobi police headquarters and getting fingerprinted. The same police who were harassing us daily.

Hassan did not win the lottery. I think I was more upset than he was. Over the summer of 2013, we lay low while plotting ways to gather my paperwork if I did get the notification to apply. Every day I checked my email for news from the State Department, but nothing came for weeks and months.

On September 21, a group of al-Shabaab terrorists attacked the Westgate Mall—the same place Hassan and I had met Dick Gordon's daughter Pamela for coffee. Inside, the mall's video surveillance cameras showed terrorists walking up and down, randomly shooting Kenyans and foreigners out for a day of shopping. Before then, their attacks were mostly around the slums, but now they had targeted the rich part of town. Over the two-day standoff, sixty-seven people were killed and many more injured.

Five miles to the east, Little Mogadishu was turning into a ghost town. People closed businesses; streets were cleared. Inside, every apartment was packed with people watching their televisions and waiting for retaliations. Many other people jammed into the mosques and prayed for peace. Within days, police in red hats invaded the neighborhood. This was the General Service Unit, a highly trained paramilitary wing. "Refugees must go back to the camps!" said a Kenya police spokesman on TV. "They must show themselves to the police officers!" Then they went straight to the mosques and started dragging people out.

Police trucks were sent into every block of Little Mogadishu. Outside our building, cops were loading Somalis into a truck like sacks of maize, just throwing them in on top of one another. Women screamed, and children cried. When the trucks filled, they drove off to the big soccer stadium at Kasarani, which had been turned into a concentration camp, and when there were no more trucks, they marched people on foot, ten miles, to the stadium.

Around midnight one night, we heard screams from downstairs, then banging at our door.

"Open the door, you terrorists, or we will break it down and kill you!"

Hassan and I knew our latch would give easily, so we decided there was no choice but to open the door. On the other side stood two policemen in red hats, but all I saw was the fist of one, thundering against my face. He hit me so hard I was blinded. Then the two of them started kicking and punching both of us. The next thing I remember was one of the cops dragging me downstairs by my collar, like they do in movies. I was screaming for my life. Hassan was right behind me. They lined us up outside in front of the police vehicle so they could see our faces in the truck lights. It was chilly and rainy, and I was shivering. My shirt was torn. I had not eaten since that morning. In my head I was imagining getting deported, having to go back to Somalia.

One by one they asked us to show IDs. When I pulled out my refugee ID, the officer threw it back in my face. He held my neck and told me to jump into the back of the truck. It was already packed with Somali refugees, there was no space, but I squeezed in and waited for the truck to move. *My American dream is dead forever,* I thought.

But then some good luck. The red hats started negotiating for money. In the end, those big-shot paramilitary cops were all about the bribe, just like the regular street cops.

Anyone who could bail himself out with cash could go back to his apartment. Hassan and I bought our way to freedom with eighty dollars that we still had from Sharon. We felt awful for the people who had no money for bribes.

The roundups and deportations went on for months, into the spring of 2014. In January, I had received a call from a BBC Radio reporter in London named Leo Hornak, who was doing a story about people who won all sorts of lotteries and wanted to interview me. So on February 4, I snuck downtown to the BBC studios and recorded an interview with him in London. In April, Leo decided to do a radio series based on my story, with me recording our Skype calls using a small digital device. But first I had to get the device—another trip downtown.

The device was a Marantz 620, about the size of a deck of cards. I could upload the recordings on our laptop. My first recording, on April 18, made Leo feel guilty for having me come downtown.

> *I'm in my room here in Little Mogadishu. The streets are under siege. The most wanted thing here is a Somali face. In the meantime, I ventured out of Little Mogadishu for the first time today. My friends, my brother, and everybody who knows me can't still believe it. On my first step out of my door, I felt butterflies in my stomach. My brother was at the door telling me not to go. It's dangerous. But I have to do an audio diary for the BBC. The equipment to record my stories is at the BBC bureau at*

downtown Nairobi. But between that audio re-
corder and me is a treacherous difficult journey.
My travel out of Little Mogadishu was like crossing
the border into another country, with heavy border
patrol. I walked along the walls of the buildings and
avoided the streets. But due to heavy rains in the
morning, the streets are ankle deep in mud. I care-
fully stepped; any car moving sends chills down my
spine. I saw bus number six headed downtown;
my eyes scanned through the passengers. There's
no single Somali here. All eyes were fixed on a
Somali face. The bus was rocking with a Jamaican
music that was more than my ears could hold. The
throbbing beat was unbearable. But it's not my ears
I care about, but my life.

Hassan and I became afraid to leave our room, even to use the bathroom downstairs. The building was by now almost empty. As the days went by, our food began to run short. We pooled our supplies with another Somali family still on the ground floor of our building—two women, one a single mom with two small boys. They had also paid bribes to stay in their place. Soon we were down to tea and some bread that was still being delivered by a Kenyan on a bicycle. We were getting desperate.

The family on the first floor ran out of money and decided to go back to Somalia. But the road home to Somalia had no promise of life. In the Kenyan countryside, gangs of robbers and rapists preyed on the returning refugees. And once they crossed the border, refugees were in the hands of al-Shabaab. That mom downstairs was more worried for her two little boys than for herself because she knew al-Shabaab would probably kidnap them and force them to join the group. But what else could she do? Starve them to death in her apartment?

I chose the path of staying in Kenya, hoping for a miracle.

With everyone else in our building gone, Hassan and I stopped leaving our apartment for anything. Classes had started, but we were not able to get to school. We covered our window and turned off all the lights after dark. We tried not to even move. We were down to a kilo of tea, some sugar, and a loaf of stale bread. Our stomachs felt like they were eating themselves inside out, and our eyes grew sticky. It was like the famine of our youth in Mogadishu, except we were in a modern African city with shops and restaurants full of people.

The police were always outside our building, eating *mandazi* and making jokes. When we had to sneak downstairs to the bathroom, we could never flush the toilet, because the police would hear it. A bucket shower was out of the question; we did not bathe for months. One night the police came up and banged on our door. Terrified, we stayed dead still, until they finally left.

Days felt like years. Weeks passed excruciatingly. Near starvation, we decided someone must venture out for supplies or die. Not only that—Ben and his family were moving to Zambia; the terror attacks in Nairobi were even chasing away Westerners. Before he left, we needed to get some cash from Sharon, through him. So one morning before daybreak, I crept out of our building for the first time in weeks with the last cash I had. The streets were empty and spooky. I jumped on a *matatu* and was off toward downtown.

Bad luck: The police were checking for Somali refugees. My heart was in my throat as the officer boarded the bus and waved his flashlight across the passengers. He noticed me right away.

"You!" he said, waving his light. "Come down!"

I descended as the bus drove away.

When I showed him my refugee document, he slapped my face and told me to sit on the side of the road.

"Ngapi?" I said in Swahili. —How much?

We argued back and forth until I handed him thirty dollars. He freed me and I caught another bus. Every minute Hassan was texting me to make sure I was fine. Any more roadblocks and I would run out of money.

Life in downtown Nairobi was carrying on as normal; there were no police in sight. As I walked up the busy Tom Mboya Street, some pedestrians veered away from me. They could tell I was Somali, but no one hassled me. Ben took me to a restaurant near his office. For the first time in weeks, I had fresh food and cold lemonade; it was heaven. He handed me six hundred dollars for food and bribes. On my way back, I bought gallons of clean water, red beans, corn, some fruits, milk, and rice. I made it back with no trouble because the police didn't care about buses going into Little Mogadishu, only coming out.

I had been building up the courage to get my Letter of Good Conduct from the police. I had no idea if my lottery number would even be called for a visa interview, but I wanted to be prepared. On May 12, a Monday, I got up early and made several calls to everyone who cared about me. I asked people to act quickly in case I got arrested. Paul sent a letter to journalists based in Kenya, and Leo emailed the Ministry of Internal Affairs. It felt good to know people were vouching for me, but I also knew that, at the police station, I would be on my own.

The Criminal Investigation Department (CID) is beyond the A2 highway that divides rich from poor. The day came that I was ready to go. I got together every letter of recommendation that I had, the U.S. senators', the journalists'. I took all my refugee papers, in duplicate, and folded cash into my pockets. I said goodbye to Hassan, walked downstairs, and opened the front door a crack. No police. I sprinted down the muddy lanes of Little Mogadishu and hopped on a bus bound north for Kiambu Road.

It had started raining again. Three officers were standing guard. Kenyans came, were searched with metal detectors, and went in. The few Somalis were forced to stand around in the rain, getting soaked. When I approached the guards, I was trembling with fear. One immediately walked toward me and yelled.

"Wait over there!" he said, and pointed to the other Somalis, making it clear we were not allowed inside. We stood in the rain for four hours. Finally a man in a dark suit came out, addressing us one by one. When it was my turn, he said, "Show me your identification."

When I pulled out my UNHCR refugee papers, he pushed me aside and moved on to the next person. I chased after him.

"Sir, please, I need the police fingerprints for my visa interview."

He turned and scowled at me. "What country are you going to?"

"United States."

He turned and moved on. I followed him down the line. Finally he turned around and said, "There's nothing I can do but take your paper and send it to UNHCR; then I have to wait for them to come back to me. It will take more than five months." In other words, he needed to verify that my documents were real. He took the duplicate of my refugee ID and ordered me to leave.

On the bus back to Eastleigh, I was almost in tears. I didn't have five months; the 2014 visa period expired in four and a half months on September 30. Besides, I didn't believe him anyway. Not that it mattered—my number had not even come up for a visa interview.

Everything changed two days later, when good luck came to my in-box. It was an email from the State Department.

> Dear DV applicant. An appointment has been
> scheduled for you at the U.S. embassy in Nairobi
> on July 22, 2014 07:30 AM. You will be required to

submit sufficient proof of identity upon arrival. If
you fail to obtain a DV-2014 visa by September 30,
2014, your registration will expire.

So this was it. I was on the list! I had sixty-nine days to
round up my paperwork. Sixty-nine days to arrange a medical exam and get transcripts from a school I could no longer
safely attend. Sixty-nine days to somehow get that police
background check. I texted all my Somali friends with the
news. They did not encourage me.

"Shit, you are crazy," wrote Yonis. "Forget about America and the lottery thing. That's not happening."

Even Hassan thought I was deceiving myself at this
point. "I think it is time to give up, Abdi," he said.

But I would not give up on my American dream until
America slammed its door shut. So my brother and I made
a pact that day: if I did not get my visa after the July 22 interview, we would join the refugees migrating north across
Sudan and into Libya, hoping for the dangerous sea passage
to Italy. We would not go back to Somalia, but we would be
done with Kenya.

First, the easy part. Africa Nazarene emailed my official
transcript. The university was sympathetic to my plight and
knew how dangerous it would be for me to travel to the
school.

May 16, a Friday, sixty-seven days until my interview. Al-
Shabaab blew up two *matatus* in Nairobi's huge Gikomba
market. At least ten died; more than seventy were injured.
The police as usual came in floods to Little Mogadishu,

and what was left of the population there. They swept buildings floor by floor, prepared to punish anyone who even looked Somali. These new police would not take bribes; they had orders to arrest refugees and even shoot them if they tried to escape. Hassan and I hid next to each other trembling in our room. We heard the voices of the cops coming up the stairs. Boots kicked at our door, but finally, they left thinking no one was there.

When we could sneak out, Hassan and I bought cheap used books from hawkers on the street, always looking to improve our English. We liked the books by successful Americans who could inspire us: scientists, inventors, and businesspeople.

I went back to the CID headquarters a few times, despite the risk, fighting my fear, to see if maybe I would get a different answer. Every time, it was the same scowling guy in the dark suit, and he did not appreciate me.

"I recognize your face," he said one time. "You are terrible! Did I not tell you to wait until I hear from the UNHCR?"

Time was running out. Thousands of lottery visas had already been approved for 2014. But the U.S. embassy in Nairobi was already scrutinizing Somali visa applicants. A young man traveling alone, with no family in the United States, was seen as highly suspect. Everywhere my hope was shrinking. I wished so badly that the embassy would read my heart instead of all these pieces of paper.

May 29, Thursday. Fifty-four days until my interview. I received a phone call from Pamela Gordon. She had heard about my troubles getting the police certificate. She said her Kenyan driver knew an officer inside the CID and maybe he could help. At least with her driver at the wheel, I could probably get inside the complex. She asked when I would want to try and I said immediately.

That afternoon, I snuck out of our room to catch a *matatu* downtown. I hailed a bus, but the driver sped past me; he did not want a Somali on board. I was freaking out, watching for cops. Finally one bus stopped. I got off downtown and met up with Pamela and her Kenyan driver. On the way to the CID, Pamela handed me two hundred dollars to bail myself out if something happened. We easily went through the gate because of the white lady and the Kenyan driver.

At the main desk we mentioned the name of the driver's friend, and I was taken by myself into his office. On his desk was the copy of my UNHCR document. The other guy had never sent it, no surprise. The man stood up from his desk. "Follow me," he said.

We turned in to a hallway of the building, a place with no surveillance cameras. "Give me eight hundred dollars," the officer said, looking around nervously.

"I don't have that much money."

"What do you have?"

I reached into my pocket and took out the two hundred dollars Pamela had given me. He snatched it from my hand and took me back into his office.

Thump! The stamp came down on my refugee document, music to my ears.

"Proceed down the hall for your fingerprints," he said.

I waited in line for a few minutes in another room. When my name was called, a lady pressed all ten of my fingers onto a pad of black ink, then onto a white sheet that said:

```
Directorate of Criminal Investigations
      Police Clearance Certificate
Remarks in Case Of Previous Record, NIL
```

"NIL." No record. That was it! I couldn't believe it. I talked to Leo that night from our room.

> *My police clearance is done! I'm looking at my ten fingers. They're all black from black ink from fingerprints. This was the only problem, I dealt with it, it's done!*

June 6, Friday. Forty-six days until my interview. I had scheduled my medical exam, which was at the Migration Health Assessment Center in northwest Nairobi, near the U.S. embassy. Another scary dash for a *matatu*.

The guard at the gate of the Migration Health Assessment Center searched me with a metal detector, then let me in. First came a blood test; then they checked my weight and height, then a quick physical. In twenty minutes, it was over. "You are all good," said the lady. "We'll send the results to the embassy. Good luck on your interview!"

June 15, a Sunday, thirty-seven days to go. Thirty masked al-Shabaab gunmen bombed a police station in the coastal Kenyan town of Malindi, stole its weapons, and went on a rampage, killing at least forty-eight people in the small village of Mpeketoni. Many of the victims were watching a World Cup match in a video hall. An al-Shabaab spokesman bragged about the attack and said they were planning more.

July 7, Monday afternoon. Fifteen days and counting. I was walking down Eighth Street when a gang of about fifty young men from the Mathare slum, armed with machetes and clubs, appeared from around the corner. Because I was a young man and, to their eyes, al-Shabaab, I was a perfect target of their anger. They chased me down the street, throwing rocks and swinging their machetes and clubs. I ran as fast as I could and threw myself headfirst into the mosque, then slammed the door shut, bolting it behind me. They knocked and kicked as I joined the other Somalis in the evening prayers. Finally they left. I am sure they would have hacked me to death, because many other Somalis were killed by these "vigilante" gangs. The murders never made the news. Still, no one in Kenya seemed to care about the lives of innocent Somalis.

July 21, the day before my interview. I washed my shirt and pants under the faucet in the bathroom downstairs. I carefully laid the shirt under my mattress to press it overnight. Leo called. "I'm not going to bed anymore," I told him.

> *I'm not going to sleep, I'm sure about that. Tomorrow's going to change my life. It's going to change my life to be the happiest person, or else it's going*

to change my life to be the most devastated man on earth, so it's these two. Tomorrow night I'm coming back to this room, breaking everything, smashing everything right here because I'm happy or I'm angry. In both situations I will break everything I know . . .

I couldn't sleep out of anticipation, but also pure fear. What if the police raided our room that night? What if I was dragged to prison, or to the airport for a deportation back to Somalia? Once you miss your interview at the embassy, it's finished. No more chances. My heart was racing.

At four thirty, I headed downstairs carrying an envelope containing my Letter of Good Conduct, the letters of support from senators and journalists, Sharon's sponsorship letter, and a printout of the emailed transcript from Africa Nazarene University. I reached the embassy gate by five. I sat on the side of the street next to the embassy building, which opened at seven. By six o'clock, a line of people arriving for their visa interviews trailed around the building. Many of them were Kenyans who had won the lottery like myself. At seven fifteen, I went through the security check, proceeded inside, and paid the $330 fee for the interview. As I waited, I saw people walking out grinning. Their visas had been approved. Others had been denied and were crying. Seeing these different emotions made me even more nervous. The stakes were so high.

My number was called to Window Nine. An African American woman with a huge smile greeted me. "Hi!"

"Good morning, ma'am," I said. So far so good; this woman was black like me and seemed nice.

"Please, can you raise your right hand and swear that everything that you will say is the truth?"

I did.

"Where did you go to college?" she asked. I told her and indicated the transcript.

"This transcript does not have a signature. Did you know that?"

I looked at it. She was right. The emailed transcript had no signature. She took out a pink piece of paper and on the bottom wrote two words, "Missing transcript." She handed it to me and said, "Sorry, I can't give you the visa. Send it to us if you can get one with a signature. And don't come back here. Just send it through DHL."

Send it through DHL?

I was speechless, frozen. All I could do was look into her eyes and beg with my own eyes for mercy. *Please change your mind*, I was praying. *Please, I need some luck today.*

But the lady didn't change her mind. She picked up her microphone and called the next number.

Dazed, I walked outside and collapsed under a tree. I was holding my head in my hands, wishing this was a nightmare I could wake up from. But the pink slip in my hand felt too real. I texted all my friends: "This is the worst day of my life." I sat there for a few more minutes, rubbing the pink slip between my hands. Then I stuffed it in my pocket, got up, and headed for the *matatu* station. The university was far and traffic was bad. As we sat stalled behind other *matatus* coughing black smoke, my heart raced and my right knee bounced. *Please move, please move.* It was four o'clock when I ran into the student affairs office. The woman behind the window said, "I'm sorry, we are closed."

"Please!" I said. "Please help me!" The lady saw my face and realized I was on fire. She signed my transcript. I dashed back downtown on another bus, crawling through heavy rush-hour traffic, arriving at the DHL office at six.

"We are closed," said the man in the office. "We close at six."

I begged and pleaded just like at the school. He let me drop the package. Within a day, the U.S. embassy would receive it, he said.

Nine days passed. I was calling the embassy every day, and every time they said, "No. We have not received the transcript."

On August 1, Leo called the U.S. embassy. He identified himself and said he was on deadline for his story and wanted to know when a decision would be made on my application. The embassy staff member had no information for him. But two hours later, I got an email from the State Department: "Your document has been received and your visa will be sent by tomorrow."

WHITE ROOMS

On the phone that night, Leo asked me what I did when I got the email. "Oh my God," I said, "I jumped off the bed and hit my head on the ceiling!"

> *It's issued! I've never had such a big smile, never ever ever. It feels like the dream has just become real. I feel like I am not a refugee. This is not a refugee that is hiding from the police. I'm an American citizen!*

Well, not exactly. But I had won the right to live and work in America. Not won. I had *earned* it. Years of practicing English, a lifetime of dodging bullets and bombs, risking death by refusing to join the militias and rebels, hiding from crooked cops, and above all, never giving up. Leo asked Hassan if he had any jealousy that only I had won. He replied,

> Actually, Leo, I tell you I don't have the least jealousy at all. If two of us get visas to get out of here, it would be even better. But if someone told me right now, "There is one visa, which one of you will take it?" I would say Abdi. Because he's new to this country and I know how we are so fearful at night. And I know how he can't sleep at night. For him to get a visa is my biggest pleasure.

Abdi American was finally going to America.

On August 8, I got a call from DHL that they had my visa and I could come collect it. By noon I walked out of that building carrying my amazing, beautiful American visa. It was Friday in downtown Nairobi, and the streets were packed with thousands of people happy that the workweek was ending. But no one was skipping like me. That day, I had to be the happiest man in Nairobi.

With my visa in hand, Sharon and Ben quickly bought me a plane ticket for Boston. My flight was on Monday at five in the morning, connecting through Addis Ababa and Frankfurt. With all of this confirmed, Leo flew into Nairobi that weekend to meet me and finish the radio documentary we were doing together. Sunday evening, my last day in Little Mogadishu, Hassan and I snuck past the police and caught a *matatu* decorated with photos of President Obama. The driver was playing Michael Jackson songs. It was perfect. Before meeting Leo at his hotel, we made a quick shopping trip. I needed luggage for my stuff—all I had were plastic shopping bags—and some clean clothes.

At nine o'clock that evening, a small Mazda car hired by the BBC staff showed up in front of the hotel. Hassan and I got in. I don't remember breathing during the twenty-minute drive to the airport. *What if a terrorist attack happens, or a bomb is thrown somewhere? They could lock down the airport and I would never be able to leave!* Leo had his microphone in my face, asking me what I was feeling like. I told him I felt like the clock was ticking. I was so nervous about the airport and if the immigration people would arrest me for being a refugee. Meanwhile, I was thinking Hassan would have to go back to that room, alone, in the dark with no company, just the brutal police.

At the airport entrance, we were stopped by the police; they peeked into the car, Leo said hi, and the Kenyan driver waved. They let us go. We all got out and entered the airport departure terminal. Leo took some pictures of Hassan and me. We hugged and said goodbye. I was so choked up I couldn't say anything to my brother. Hassan told me to stay strong. His last words were "Remember to support Mom!"

With that, I proceeded inside. The Kenya immigration officer looked at my visa, stamped my refugee documents, and waved me through. So easy with the right piece of paper. Hassan and Leo decided to wait at a cafeteria inside the airport until the flight took off, to make sure I departed without being arrested.

It was ten o'clock when I sat down at the gate for the long wait until my flight. I was the first passenger there. I sat alone looking around the airport, watching people come and go. After a few hours, many other people joined me in the wait. Finally, our boarding was announced. I had a window seat. When we took off, the sun was just rising above the horizon. My American dream was now becoming real life, and it seemed like everything in my past life was becoming a dream that I needed to wake up from.

After a stop in Ethiopia, we landed in Frankfurt, where I had to change planes. That airport was so huge I freaked out for a moment trying to connect with my flight to Boston. We had to take a bus to the departure gate. Again, I boarded the biggest airplane I had ever seen. Again, I had a window seat. An American lady with her teenage daughter sat next to me. After takeoff they shut their eyes and acted like the flight was boring. I was awake; I could not take my eyes off the window and the screen in front of me that showed where we were. At some point we were flying over the United Kingdom; I looked down, and I could see water and what seemed like a city. Then all was blue for hours and hours.

My heart was beating fast as the plane banked over downtown Boston and descended to Logan Airport. My face was glued to the window as I looked at the skyscrapers of America, then the blue waters of the Atlantic. Even though we were going down, I felt like I was going up to heaven. When the wheels bumped on the runway, I couldn't control myself. "I am in America!" I shouted.

Even the bored lady next to me smiled. "Welcome!" she said.

As we taxied to the gate, I thought of my brother in Kenya, my mom on the dusty streets of Mogadishu waiting for the good news, my friends in the tea shop in Little Mogadishu who applied for the visa lottery when I forced them, all the while assuring me it was hogwash. But I had no thought of saying, "I told you so." I was overwhelmed with joy, tears melting down my cheeks.

Exiting the plane felt like a historic moment. People poured out of the flight; they were in some sort of a hurry. It seemed like everyone knew what to do and where to go. I just stood there and watched everything. I looked around the immigration hall—so far, no Hollywood, no Disney World, no Statue of Liberty or Harvard University, not even Walmart or KFC. I saw people who looked a little like Bruce Willis, Sylvester Stallone, Eddie Murphy, Oprah, or Tom Cruise, and I couldn't take my eyes off them. But I was not the only stranger there. A group of Asians speaking a strange language were lined up in front of me. People of other colors were everywhere. A black man right behind me in the line was glued to his phone.

"Hi!" I said.

"Hello." To my surprise he had a thick African accent.

"I'm from Somalia. Where are you from?"

"Nigeria," he replied, barely looking up from his phone.

It was the first time in my entire life I saw a Nigerian. He told me he had lived in America for ten years.

So many different kinds of people in America! As the line moved on slowly, I gazed up at the huge television screens flashing the news:

. . . actor Robin Williams has committed suicide . . .

. . . protests erupted in Ferguson, Missouri, after the killing of a black man . . .

It was a police officer who shot the man, but people were protesting, taking to the streets. Although many Americans might not be happy with things in the United States, to me the protests were just a sign of freedom that people can get out onto the streets and show their unhappiness. Kenyan police would have killed Somalis who dared to protest in Little Mogadishu.

When it was my turn, an officer asked me some questions and handed me a form to fill out. I had to choose between being African, African American, Hispanic, or Caucasian. This threw me at first because I had never thought of myself as African. In Somalia we identify ourselves by our tribes.

An officer led me into a room where an American lady took my fingerprints and photo. She said my official green card would arrive at my address in Maine. "Welcome to the United States!" she said.

When I finally walked through the doors from the immigration hall into the terminal, I flinched from the sudden rush of activity. People were everywhere, holding signs, wheeling suitcases, hugging relatives. Now I was really in

America! Then I saw Sharon McDonnell and her daughter, Natalya, both trying to catch sight of me; they were holding a sign that said "Abdi Iftin." Sharon had straight shoulder-length blond hair, and Natalya a dark ponytail. We met and I stooped to hug them. Both were so much shorter than I imagined, not like Americans in the movies or the marines in Mogadishu. They looked up at me with huge smiles. "Welcome!" said Sharon. "Let's take you to your new home."

We left through a huge revolving door to the curbside. My first moment breathing the fresh air of America! Except it smelled like diesel fumes right there, not much different from Africa. I kept my eyes fixed on Sharon, this person who had changed my life forever. I was looking at her like she was superhuman—not superhuman like the comic-book heroes I saw in movies but in some other way that was maybe even stronger. We took some pictures; I bounced from place to place asking for shots.

In truth I was also scared. A Somali living with a white family could be known as a converted person, someone who left the culture and Islam. What would my family and friends think? What if Sharon had a dog? What if the dog licks and sniffs me? How would I behave?

We got into the car. Sharon and Natalya showed me how to buckle up. "You need to do this every time you get in a car," said Sharon. "It's the law." I couldn't believe I was in a place where people actually obeyed laws. Also, I had never seen a woman driving in my life, except in movies.

We left the airport on a busy divided road out of Boston heading up to Maine. I saw lots of big stores and restaurants.

I saw a restaurant called Kowloon shaped like some kind of South Pacific island hut; it looked larger than the huge Isbaheysiga mosque in Mogadishu. Next came some kind of cowboy place with a neon cactus sign as tall as buildings in Nairobi. I kept thinking, *Here I am in a car in America with friends who helped me and my family, even though we are not in their tribe or do not practice the same religion.* This aspect of humanity was very touching to me. I sat quietly as we drove and tried to make sense of it.

Night fell slowly and late, it was past eight o'clock and still some light. We kept driving through the twilight, zooming by more huge shops and parking lots, now blazing under blue lights. Soon, there were fewer lights and buildings, more trees. I rolled down my window to get a better flavor of America, the cool late-summer wind over my face. When we pulled off the highway for gas and some food, I ordered a cheeseburger for my first American dinner. With a full tank we were off on the road again, this time Natalya driving. Sharon talked about the weather, how the trees will change colors, how snow will fall, Thanksgiving, Christmas. They already had plans for all these events.

Finally we pulled up in their driveway. Sure enough, at the door we were greeted by their dog, named Lacy. She jumped all over me, licking. Dog saliva is considered impure to Muslims, so now I definitely felt butterflies in my stomach. I froze with fear.

"She's friendly," said Natalya. "She's just excited."

The two cats, Tigger and Jasmin, did not even bother waking up from their naps. But the dog followed me upstairs to my room and jumped on the bed. When Sharon and Natalya said good night, I wondered if the dog would leave me. She stayed there. I couldn't sleep with a dog in my room—it was too scary—so finally I got her out and shut the door.

I was too excited to sleep, but fortunately the morning came soon: five o'clock and it was already light. America seemed quiet, not like the streets of Mogadishu or Little Mogadishu. I watched the light filter into my room from the large window and looked outside. A herd of deer grazed like camels just beyond the cars. The sun appeared between the branches where squirrels were playing. The window faced east; now I knew which way to pray.

The walls of my room were painted white and blue, strange colors for walls, which are always the color of mud in Africa. The ceiling was so flat and perfect; how do they do that? The house was built in the nineteenth century, but to me it looked brand-new. There was a dial on the wall to adjust the heat. The room was obsessively neat: somebody's clothes hung perfectly in the closet, not draped over a frayed clothesline like in an African hut, and pictures of birds and flowers in gold frames hung on the wall. A sculpture of Buddha sat quietly on the floor. I didn't know who Buddha was, but I soon learned Sharon and her family believed in Buddhism.

This room seemed way too big for just me, probably double the size of the room my brother and I shared in Nairobi.

I got dressed and went down to see the family.

"Let's help you fix your first American breakfast," said

Sharon. The breakfast would be milk, eggs, and toast. They had lots of eggs from their chickens. "And also there's lots of leftovers in the refrigerator," she said. I did not know Americans ate leftovers. The refrigerator was packed with leftover soup, rice, eggs, pasta, juice, sauce, everything. Drawers were full of food. There were crackers, granola, dog food, and cat food. There was food everywhere in the kitchen. The living room was full of books and magazines. There was a big red couch to sit on and read. A nice porch and a big Apple computer. I went on and updated my Facebook posts. This time I didn't need Photoshopped pictures of me in America; I used actual pictures we took at Logan the night before. My friends commented with questions like "Are u living with a Christian family?" "Are you going to convert?"

My orientation started with using the oven and the toaster. I had seen kitchens in movies, but I never thought I would use such things. I learned how to warm things from the "fridge" using the microwave. Soon I learned about the dishwasher, the clothes washer, the dryer, which food goes where in the refrigerator. I learned to leave tips at restaurants. And I was learning new English words every day, starting with "closet," "vacuum," "the vet," "chicken coop," "the barn," "mowing," and all different types of food.

I met Gib, Sharon's husband, the most easygoing person I have ever come across. He is short and thin, and his deep blue eyes miss nothing. He seems to think very carefully before he says anything, and he likes things to be in order. Gib teaches at the University of New Hampshire in Manchester.

Before he went out to "run errands," he asked me, "Is there anything you want me to get you from the grocery store?" He spent his leisure time doing things around the house. He would disappear into the basement and work on electric wires, or out to the yard putting up a fence. In Africa it is unusual for a man to know how to cook, but Gib cooked great meals—fried rice, guacamole, and the most delicious cakes.

I could not get a job in the United States until my Social Security card and green card arrived. While I waited, the McDonnell-Parrish family offered me jobs in their house. I cut and stacked firewood for the winter. I fed the horse, cleaned the stall and the chicken coop, watered plants, cleared fallen branches from the driveway. I spent all day working outside and came in only for a quick break for lunch of a sandwich and some orange juice. They paid me ten dollars an hour. I worked every day of the week and earned over six hundred dollars, but it went fast. After buying a bike, some new clothes, work gloves, and goggles for splitting firewood, I had enough left for my daily treat of doughnuts and coffee at Dunkin' Donuts. At night I would relax by browsing on Netflix and watching movies.

I woke up every day enjoying work, and there was always something to do; even clearing spiderwebs from the barn was a job the family had long wanted to do. Natalya was scared of spiders, but years earlier I had cleared spiderwebs for Falis in her video shack, so I was prepared.

Natalya was a senior at Yarmouth High School, but this was still summer break, so she and I walked miles every day through town. As we walked, I waved to drivers passing by, and they waved back or smiled. Natalya told me some people in America are racists. I was not sure what racism was; all I knew was hatred and bigotry from Kenya, and that was not about skin color. She took me around to meet the neighbors so everyone would know me and not dial 911 when I walked around. *Why would they dial the police when they saw me?* That didn't make sense to me. Regardless, we played soccer and video games and went on shopping trips. Natalya had not had someone at home to hang out with since her older brother, Morgan, moved to California; now she again enjoyed doing things with a brother. One day she posted a photo of me on social media holding my favorite chocolate chip vanilla ice cream, describing me as her older, adopted brother. My Somali friends started calling me on the phone, in shock. One said, "Have you lost your mind? You can't make her a sister unless she is Muslim."

Weeks passed. Fall came. The sun was setting and rising more like in Somalia around six, but it was getting much colder than it ever does in Somalia. The leaves on the trees were turning golden and red; I had never seen such colors on trees. In the house, people talked about the weather, food, vacations, books, and movies. There was always something going on. Soon, Thanksgiving was coming. When the day finally arrived, we had ten people around the table, mostly relatives. Everyone wanted to meet me, the new member of the McDonnell-Parrish family. We had turkey, sweet potato soufflé, apple pie, ice cream—so much food. I almost forget what it was like to be so hungry you are in physical agony. Almost. I couldn't believe I was sitting at a large table surrounded by white people with glasses of beer in their hands, and I was like one of them. They talked about American football, TV shows they had seen, and hiking and other trips they did. They talked about their animals, their families. I watched and learned. I talked about my story and my new life in Maine.

I watched from across the street as the mailman dropped envelopes into the box every day. I'd run to grab the mail as soon as he came, checking to see if my name was on anything. I was waiting for my green card.

It finally arrived. The card had a computer image of me, the picture they took at Logan Airport, next to a picture of the Statue of Liberty. It said UNITED STATES OF AMERICA and PERMANENT RESIDENT. Me and the Statue of Liberty, permanent residents.

My Social Security card came soon after, which meant I could work and buy a car. Most important, it was the first step to my goal of becoming a citizen of the United States of America.

...

Meanwhile, back in Somalia, neighbors poured into my mom's shack in the Eelasha camp to congratulate her on my arrival in the United States. They treated her like she'd hit the jackpot. Distant relatives who had always avoided Mom were practically moving in, waiting for her to promise them something. But she had not received a penny from me. She expected money the day after I arrived, but weeks passed and I had not sent a dollar, because I could not find a job, and I had already spent the little money I earned from housework. Sharon and Gib were so generous in giving me a place to stay and free meals, but once I had cleaned everything around their property, there wasn't much more work I could do for them.

No one in Africa believed me. When I spoke to my mom on the phone, she was deaf to my complaints about the lack of work in America, where money was supposed to grow on trees. She thought I had become arrogant, that my newfound wealth had changed me. I had no way to convince her that life could also be hard in America, just in different ways. But her problems were bigger than mine; she and Nima needed money to survive and buy food. I stayed up all night, looking online for any work that I thought I could do. I tried warehouses, laundries, bakeries, bathroom cleaning, floor mopping, and many other jobs. Many ended up being too far away from Yarmouth, and I had no car or even a driver's license. So I had to limit my search to jobs within walking or biking distance.

I walked around town, visiting neighbors, asking if they needed someone to work in their yard or help with anything. I visited local farms to see if they wanted help. Some of the online applications for warehouse jobs got back to me for interviews. The bosses smiled. They all turned me down. Was it my English? Was it because I was new to the country? I did not have previous work experience here in the United States, something they always asked about. I had scrambled to work and make money since I was a child in Somalia, trying to buy food and water for my family, yet I had no résumé or references.

My fears of unemployment grew stronger after every interview. I was really struggling to understand how America works. I was ready to do any kind of work, the dirtiest jobs, but still I could find nothing.

Maine is home to about ten thousand Somali immigrants, most of them living in Lewiston, an old textile mill town in central Maine and the home of Bates College. Many others live in Portland, the state's largest city. The Somali refugees get help from resettling agencies and charities that give them money for the first eight months and assign caseworkers who help them find jobs and ease into their new lives. But I was not technically a refugee. And while Sharon and Gib were doctors who traveled the world helping to fight diseases, they were not social workers trained to help an African immigrant navigate America.

Also there were no Somalis in Yarmouth. In Lewiston and Portland, Somalis can ride buses around town. In Yarmouth at the time, there were no buses, so I rode a bike around, asking every business on Main Street if it had any jobs. People would stare at me like they had never seen a black neighbor. Children looked startled; they would hide behind their parents' legs and point. It felt strange to be so different. Somalis don't look like Kenyans, but it's a matter of degrees. Here I was made to feel like a space alien. I stopped by the Dunkin' Donuts, Romeos Pizza, several horse farms, the laundry, even the transfer station. But no one had a job.

At dinnertime one evening in November, the house phone rang. It was Christine, one of Sharon's friends. She told her that a local home insulation company was seeking men who could do tough work. Winter was coming and the demand for warm insulation was growing. I emailed the manager, and we arranged an interview that week.

The leaves of the trees were turning dull brown and falling as I walked to the interview. It was getting dark even earlier and getting even colder. The manager looked at my green card. "What is your name?" he asked. It was on the card, but I guess he couldn't tell my first name from my last name.

"Abdi," I said.

"Forgive me if I pronounce your name wrong," he said. "You look good, strong and energetic; we need guys like you, *Abbi*. This job is dealing with heavy material and climbing roofs. Are you okay with heights?"

I told him I didn't have a problem with heights and that I really needed the job.

"We pay eleven dollars an hour," he said. "We might increase the pay if your work is good." He seemed like he was apologizing for the pay, but to me it was great, the most I had ever earned in my life. He asked if I could work on weekends. I said I could work anytime day or night. I walked out of that building on air.

■ ■ ■

Monday morning, November 17, was my first day on the job. When my alarm went off at four o'clock in the morning, I dressed warm, in layers of silk and wool. I had my usual breakfast of eggs, milk, and toast. Everyone else in the house was asleep. It was a forty-five-minute walk to work and I headed out, with my new craft knife tucked in my belt, my staple gun in my back pocket, and my hard hat on. I walked through the woods; all was quiet and silent except the scared deer that dashed when they heard me coming.

"Welcome on board," said the manager when I arrived. He introduced me to the guys I would be working with. They were all big, muscular Maine guys in dirty clothes and big construction boots. Whenever they talked, they cursed. They wrestled and punched each other. Except for being white, they reminded me of Somali militiamen. They carried themselves the same aggressive way. But I was so happy to have the job that I ignored my fear.

The crew boss, Joey, told the workers my name, but they all struggled with it. *Eddy, Abey, Abbdey.* I told them whatever was fine. I could barely understand their thick Maine accents anyway. Until now I had been proud of my English, but they kept correcting my mistakes and laughing at my accent, so I felt humiliated and different. To them, I was a strange African man, not the American I wanted to be.

Joey assigned me to work with Milton and Sean, experienced workers who had been with the company for more than ten years. Milton read the instructions for the day's job. It was a commercial building, six floors; we would "batt" the walls and the ceilings with fiberglass insulation. We were called the batting squad. Both Milton and Sean were big, strong guys with tattoos all over their bodies.

Sean had piercings in his nose and lower lip; Milton was missing some front teeth.

I loaded the heavy rolls of insulation into the big delivery truck from "the shop," which is what we called the Yarmouth warehouse. Heavy bundles of fiberglass sat everywhere. Milton used one hand rolling the whole bundle to the truck. I struggled with two hands. While I loaded one, he loaded three. The tiny strands of fiberglass got all over my clothes; even with gloves, a face mask, and goggles I was itching. The three of us, the batting squad, climbed into the cab and drove off, Milton behind the wheel.

As soon as the truck left the shop, both men reached into their duffel bags and took out marijuana. "Do you smoke, dude?" Milton asked me.

"No," I said. I had never smoked marijuana or even seen it. I'd never even smoked a cigarette. As they puffed their weed, the smoke filled the cabin. "It smells bad," I said. They just laughed, looked at me, and said something I couldn't understand. They spoke so quickly and with sarcasm that was new to me. They talked about their wives, going to clubs, drinking beer, smoking weed, cars, winning the lottery, pizza, and professional wrestling. I sat next to them in silence, trying to absorb and learn their culture, looking out at the trees and buildings. We talked about Africa. To them, Africa was one big country of naked people who eat snakes. More monkeys and lions than people. I told them that we have highways, airplanes, and cars, which surprised them.

The walls of the building were made of metal studs, not

mud or blocks. It didn't seem very sturdy to me. While Milton and Sean smoked cigarettes and drank Red Bull outside the building, I started unloading the fiberglass batts and carrying them to the upper floors. I was breathing heavily and my goggles fogged up, so I could barely see. I wondered, were these guys just leaving all the heavy lifting to me? Finally, Milton and Sean put on their favorite rock and roll music blasting all over the building and got to work. They showed me how to cut open the bundles of insulation, then how to put on stilts so we could batt the ceiling. Sean and Milton didn't bother to wear masks or goggles, but they told me I should wear them because I was new and not used to the fiberglass.

My first paycheck was a happy day; I had earned $400. Because I was living with Sharon and Gib and still had no car, my personal expenses were small, and I was able to send $340 to my mom. I was so proud as I walked into Portland's halal market, which was the unofficial *hawala* money-transfer station. I handed over my cash to the guy behind the counter, he took an extra six dollars for every hundred as a fee. Then he communicated by computer with the *hawala* kiosk in Mogadishu, where my mom went in and claimed the money.

She was so happy, she bought a goat and slaughtered it, cooked a pot of rice, and threw a party for the neighbors. Macalin Basbaas came and enjoyed the meal. My mom said he prayed for me: "May God keep him safe and working hard."

...

Every day we batted different houses and buildings in different towns. Ten miles, twenty miles, and sometimes as far as eighty miles. We had to finish batting a whole house within the same day, so we moved fast. Lunch break was thirty minutes. Milton and Sean ate doughnuts, sometimes burgers they brought with them. I always sought a clean place and prayed. They both would come look at me bowing my head and reciting the Koran.

"What are you doing?" Milton asked me.

During the prayer, I am not supposed to speak, so I was quiet and answered when I finished. "I was praying."

Milton picked up his phone and called everyone else who worked at the company and even his wife. He made fun of the whole thing. "This dude bows and says he's praying," he said with a laugh.

I had to tell them that I am Muslim; I have to pray five times a day. "They got Muslims in Africa?" Sean asked. Of course they thought all Muslims look like Osama bin Laden.

After work, Milton and Sean would stop at a convenience store to buy beer and cigarettes. Often they would ask to borrow money from me until the next payday. I always gave them a few dollars when they asked, but they never paid me back. I wasn't sure if it would be polite to remind them on payday.

One day on the job, my hard hat disappeared. Another day my staple gun, then my winter coat. When I asked what could have happened, Milton laughed and said, "That's what happens when you're new here." The boss said he couldn't do anything. I had to buy a new hard hat and a new staple gun from the shop. I had no idea who was stealing my stuff until one day I found my hard hat in the back of Milton's pickup truck. The same guys I'd been working with for months, and when I asked, they said nothing! It was humiliating, and it felt as if my American dream was shrinking.

Looking back, I think the guys on the batting squad were racist; but at that point, I hadn't been in America long enough to know about that. But it did feel like something I understood very well: the tribalism of Somalia. I have heard Americans complain that Africans bring on their own problems with their tribal feuds, and there is some truth to that. But these Maine guys had a tribe too. Maybe they didn't call themselves Darod or Hawiye, but it was a tribe, and I definitely was not a member.

I asked Joey to put me on a different batting squad, and I was told to work with a guy named Tom. He was respectful to me, rolling down his window when smoking. He had been to prison several times, due to drugs, and he said he wanted to stop. He wanted to go to college, and he asked me questions about my life back in Africa. I told him about the wars and the death and the escapes, and he shook his head in disbelief. "Dude!" he said. "I grew up with an abusive dad and I spent seven years in prison, but that's nothing compared to your shit."

Tom and I got along well. I felt it was safe to leave my

things in his truck. He wanted to see the world outside the United States; he wanted to explore. He told me he liked watching National Geographic TV shows. He watched shows about the Maasai Mara and Serengeti national parks in Kenya and Tanzania. We talked about lions, hyenas, and wildebeests. I told him stories about my mom and dad facing lions in real life. I liked Tom.

There was always a radio on the work site, always blaring rock and roll, blues, or country music. The guys could name all the bands and artists, but they didn't know anything about American history. They couldn't name many presidents except the most recent ones or George Washington, and they didn't know about the Black Hawk Down incident in Mogadishu, even though there were pictures online. They had no idea where Somalia was.

Many of the guys on the batting squad gave each other rides home. Milton gave Sean a ride, and Tom picked up two other people. I asked if someone could give me a ride home, and Milton said I would have to pay him gas money. None of the other guys gave him gas money, but he wanted twenty dollars a week from me. I told him I was happy to walk home, even though I was so tired and dirty after work.

So I had to walk home, up Main Street, looking like some homeless guy in my filthy work clothes and covered in pink fiberglass threads. Fortunately, the people of Yarmouth got to know me and realized I was just a hardworking guy. When I got home, I took off my rough clothes, took a warm shower, dressed up nice, and walked back toward

Main Street. People waved and smiled. I started to feel like part of the community and not just the outsider like I felt at work.

One night at the dinner table, the weather news was on; there was a brutal and early winter storm coming to Maine, they said. A "northeaster." People were instructed to drive slow; schools were canceled. Everyone around the table had been preparing. There were shovels ready at the front door. Wood was thrown into the burning stove.

"We'll have to give you a ride to work tomorrow," said Gib. "It will be hard to walk in the storm." I went to bed at seven o'clock as usual and woke up at four, when it was still dark outside. Out the window of my room I saw my first snow! I noticed the flakes falling silently, not like rain. The sky was glowing white and hazy.

I got dressed and went outside to help Gib shovel the walkways. Snow covered the cars and roofs. The roads were hardly recognizable. My hands turned numb from the cold, even with gloves. All day at work I was freezing because there was not yet any heat in the buildings where we were installing the batts. I needed warmer clothes.

It felt good to come home from work in the evening for a warm shower and a tasty dinner. I turned up the heat, browsed Netflix, and watched lots of movies, one every night before bed.

Every night after a great movie, I buried myself underneath a warm blanket and thought about my past life, the tough times, the near-death escapes. My heart warmed with the knowledge that I was far away from that pain, even as I worried for my family. But waking up in the morning for work, I had to face another freezing day on the batting squad.

One day the manager of the company called me into his office to tell me I was getting a raise to twelve dollars an hour. He put me on the night shift with a batting squad insulating a new school building on an island off the coast of Portland. Every evening we took our truck out to the island on a ferry, then worked all night as more and more snow fell.

All of my coworkers liked to go hunting; they shot deer and turkeys and sometimes even moose and bears. They talked all the time about guns and what kinds of guns they liked best. I knew lots of guns too, but not the kind they took hunting. Of course I always saw lots of weapons in Hollywood movies but didn't really understand how much Americans thought about shooting guns. It wasn't just hunting; all over the news that winter were stories of black Americans getting shot by police. There was so much talk of racism; I didn't understand how much this existed in the United States. Every day was a new surprise.

I couldn't believe Americans were scared for their lives in their own homes until I heard stories like that. I slept in my big white room peacefully, with no sounds of gunfire anywhere around or police kicking down my door for a bribe.

Then we had a gun incident at work. Jimmy, one of the older guys working at the company, was fired for smoking weed inside the office. His coworkers made fun of him for getting fired. But the next morning, Jimmy returned to the shop with a rifle in his hand, threatening to spray bullets on us. It was a Friday and payday, so all the guys had been in a good mood. But the happy day turned into a frantic game of hide-and-seek as we scattered behind stacks of insulation. The cops soon arrived and managed to get the gun from Jimmy before they arrested him. It was still so early in the morning, and most of Yarmouth was still asleep. Until then, the only white Americans I had seen with guns were those marines in Mogadishu, and they always pointed their weapons away from us. I had no idea Americans turned guns on each other like Somali militiamen, and this left me scared and deeply confused.

...

Months passed and the winter finally ended. The warm weather felt so good, but I realized I had been in America almost a year and without much progress. I was trying so hard to fit in, but I had so much to learn. One day I left the stove on—I forgot you have to turn it off, as it's not like a cook fire that burns out. Sharon and Gib were so patient and kind, but my pride made me embarrassed to make mistakes. Sometimes I went upstairs, lay in my bed, and remembered the good old days when thinking about America was heavenly. I was realizing nothing is easy, even in America.

Somalis are pretty reserved around strangers; until you know someone, it's considered best to listen respectfully and be quiet. But most Americans speak their minds right away. They are not afraid of starting a conversation. I struggled for months to gain such confidence.

I didn't want to admit this to myself, but I was also suffering from post-traumatic stress disorder. Since then, I have learned that virtually all Somali refugees have some version of this. I would wake up at night in a sweat, having nightmares, which only made me more tired at work. When I wasn't working, I spent more and more time up in my room watching movies and surfing the Internet. I talked on the phone with Hassan a lot and I found peace talking to him about life, even though he was still at the mercy of the brutal Kenyan police. He kept telling me that everything would work out fine. Hassan was preparing to marry his new sweetheart—another Somali refugee, a woman he had met in Little Mogadishu who was selling fruits and milk on the street. Together we planned his wedding over the phone. We had fun talking about the music and food he would have.

I found myself missing all my African friends and our shared language and culture. I missed drinking Somali tea and sitting around on floor mats, eating dinner with our hands, no forks, no spoons. I realized that as horrible as my life was in Africa, I was homesick. I knew I could not reasonably go back to Kenya even for a visit, much less Somalia, but I longed to see more of America. I wanted to see the America from movies, where black people in sneakers play basketball on the side of the street. I heard that a group of immigrants played soccer every weekend in Portland, and I decided to join them.

Gib gave me a ride down to the pitch on Back Cove. I couldn't believe what I saw—Iraqis, Burundis, Rwandans, Somalis, Latin Americans, and other people, all playing soccer together. I heard Spanish, French, Swahili, Somali, Kinyarwanda, Arabic, and more. But together we all spoke English, our one common language. I had no idea all these people lived in Maine! About a third of the players were female, white American women who loved soccer. They played hard and scored goals, roaming the pitch as defenders, strikers, and even midfielders. I'd never seen anything like this either.

I joined up quickly and had an amazing day, even scoring a goal. We played rough, lots of tackling and tripping, stuff that would definitely draw penalties in a professional match. But at the end of the day, it was handshakes and congratulations to the winners, and so much fun. As much as I loved my family in Yarmouth, I decided I needed to be close to these people too.

· 16 ·

RESPECT

Through a friend of Sharon's, I was introduced to Kamal, a guy who ran an agency in Portland that helped settle new Somali immigrants, most of whom suffered from trauma and emotional stress and spoke no English. Kamal took me to the main mosque in town, and I couldn't believe that most of the Somalis I met there had cars, jobs, and their own homes. Within a week, I said warm goodbyes to my new American family, quit my job on the batting squad, and moved into an apartment in Portland with four other Somali guys. The second-floor apartment was in a complex of several nearly identical buildings, spread out on a winding road amid lots of trees, like a suburban street. Many of the apartments had Somali and other refugees, or really poor Americans, and were publicly subsidized. We paid the market rate because we all had green cards and could work.

My plan was to get a job in Portland; until then I would pay my four-hundred-dollar monthly rent and utilities out of savings.

It sounded like a TV show: five Somali guys in a small Maine apartment. There was Kamal, the only one of us who had already become an American citizen. Burhan and Liban worked at Walmart and the Shaw's grocery store; Gedi was a taxi driver. The apartment had only two bedrooms and one bathroom, but we just spread out mattresses and slept all over the floor, taking turns in the bathroom. I was in charge of making breakfast, usually Somali sour pancakes called *anjara*, with peas and some cubed lamb or goat from the halal market. For lunch everyone was off at work; dinner was the Somali version of beans and rice known as *ambulo*, drizzled with sesame or olive oil and a little sugar. Of course we ate on the floor, with our hands, just like in Africa. We laughed so hard, wrestled, drove together to soccer games and the mosque.

My roommates had all been in Maine for several years, making me the new guy in town. But I was surprised how little American culture they had absorbed. I would play the latest hip-hop songs on my phone while I cooked, but they preferred to listen to Arabic chants called *nasheeds* that are popular back in Somalia. No one seemed to have the same passion I felt for America. Kamal was the only one who knew English fluently.

I said to them, "Ten years in America, why don't you learn English? You could get better jobs! Cashiers make more than shelf stockers, but they need to speak English.

And you could have fun on the weekend, going to movies and parties." But Gedi, Liban, and Burhan felt like they were just biding their time until they could return to Somalia. They checked the Somali news every day, hoping peace would come. Some had returned home at least twice for visits, and they talked about enjoying camel milk and camel meat, which you can't find in Maine. Gedi's dad was the chief of a village in southern Somalia, and Gedi hoped to inherit the crown when his dad stepped down. Whenever he visited Somalia, the villagers gave him a royal reception. It must have been hard to come back to Portland and pick up passengers at the bus terminal.

All my roommates were supporting their families back home. Most of what they did not spend on their own small expenses went back to Somalia. There were always too many people to support and not enough money. Every week was the same: you got paid on Friday; you sent whatever money was left over from the last week to your relatives in Somalia or Kenya. Life was one paycheck at a time, so different from my American friends who always talked about their future goals. They wanted to go to college, get a good job, save money to buy a house or travel, the usual things. For most Somalis in Maine, the only future goal besides going home was to have money left over at the end of the week so your family in Somalia could boil some beans and maize.

My roommates were members of either the Hawiye or the Darod clan. My Rahanweyn clan does not have much of a presence here in Maine, and often I felt disconnected. Many Somalis I met asked me about my clan. When I told them Rahanweyn, they would ask me what I was doing in Maine; there are more Rahanweyn in Minnesota or Seattle, they said. But I told them I was not here to reunite with my tribe, I was here to be American. That sounded like a crime to them—to abandon your clan and become an American! To them, you could not be Somali without having a clan.

Still, others I had met along the way offered another perspective. Shannon and Tina, the Americans I befriended while volunteering for the Afya Njema project in Kenya, were proudly spiritual but not religious. They lived with their boyfriends, even though their families had big houses. They preferred to live their own way. That individual liberty was such a new concept to me, to most Africans, and it was scary but exciting. It got me thinking that this is a great nation where you can be anyone, as long as you can learn the language and customs. That was my task, and I worked at it every day. So many figures of speech to memorize! Someone asked me, "What is your apartment situation like?" I started describing the kitchen, the bathroom, the location. Then he said he meant who were my roommates, how much was the rent, and so on. The "situation."

I have always been fast to learn languages, but now I was finding that American customs and culture were much harder to absorb, and in these cases my language skills often failed me. Discussions about American music, sports, TV shows, food, or breeds of dogs just made me sit there like an idiot. Sometimes I felt all I could talk about were my own life stories. People appreciated hearing them, but

I also wanted to feel like I belonged here and could talk about American things. So I vowed to keep learning.

I was often invited by my American friends to go hiking, skiing, and other fun weekend things, and I always accepted. When I returned from the movies or hikes or other fun things to my apartment, I would recount my activities. My roommates asked if I had prayed during all the fun. When I said no, they yelled at me for becoming too American. My roommates also thought outdoor activities were stupid.

"You have abandoned your faith for a hike in the woods!"

"Why bother building a camp in the wilderness when you can sleep in your freshly made bed?"

"We came here from refugee camps. Camping is not fun!"

"We hiked hundreds of miles through the bush into Kenya; now we have cars, we don't need to hike!"

Birthdays were another strange concept to my roommates. Everyone in our apartment except me was born on January 1. In Somalia no one cares about age. People are born and die. Period. My roommates thought I was crazy for picking June 20 as my birthday, but why was that any worse than picking January 1? Meanwhile my family in Yarmouth put a huge effort into celebrating my birthday every year, with a cake and candles and a big dinner. And my American friends on Facebook always left me warm birthday wishes. On June 20, I always felt like I was born an American.

...

The Somali community in Maine is run by sheikhs and imams, who lead the prayers at the mosques. In Portland, the Muslim Community Center is where everyone gathers to pray, especially on Friday. Sheikh Ahmed is one of the top leaders, and he also owns a halal market. One day he delivered a speech to the men.

"We've got a problem in the Muslim community in Maine. So many of our young men are abandoning the culture. Some even live with white families! Some are dating white non-Muslim women; some are drinking alcohol. This is a huge problem. We ask for your support to do counseling for these young men and help them return to the word of Allah."

The sheikhs in Portland told people to do the same things they expected in Somalia: women should not go outside without their husbands, men should wear ankle-length clothes and a beard, and on and on. But here in the United States they couldn't force people, especially me. I had memorized the Koran; I knew and respected my religion. But still my roommates and I got into heated debates about the message the Koran sends. To them the message was clear: you must be a God-fearing person and stay away from anything that could distract you from the five daily prayers.

I came to see that my roommates would never assimilate, and they were not alone. Like the first Italians or Chinese or Slovaks who came to America, the first-generation Somalis, many of whom were already old when they arrived, were too set in their language, culture, and religion. It would be the next generation to call themselves American, and they were the ones giving their parents headaches by dating before marriage or even going to clubs.

Meanwhile, an army of caseworkers, many of them working for Christian organizations, rallied to help refugees navigate this strange new country. There was an opening for an interpreter on the website of a nonprofit agency. People were needed in hospitals and courts who could help Somalis talk to lawyers, doctors, and judges, and translate anything that might be unfamiliar. I quickly applied and a day later got a call from a woman in its language department. "Oh, your English is good," she said. I went for an interview, filled out the usual forms. A week later I was hired, but before I could start the job, I was sent to take a required interpretation course at Southern Maine Community College.

My classmates were all foreigners from Burundi, Rwanda, Iraq, and even Russia. We were taught the medical and legal terms, the dos and don'ts of being an interpreter. They said we must never interact with clients outside the job; that would be unprofessional. I learned about the U.S. health care system, medical terminology, basic human biology, systems, and treatments.

My first job was at Community Dental, translating for Farhan, an elderly Somali man who had been in Portland for two years. Farhan had a bullet wound on his head from a gunfight in Somalia. I sat across from him, next to the dentist, translating what the doctor said as well as what Farhan said. In the next few weeks, I got more and more assignments, traveling to Maine Medical Center, Mercy Hospital, the Department of Health and Human Services, Opportunity Alliance, Portland high schools, job fairs, the courts, and many other places around southern Maine.

I soon realized it would be impossible to always maintain a professional distance from the clients. Many times they just wanted to ask me about my tribe or my background, and I felt it would be rude not to converse with them. Also, they often had so many questions about the law or the medical treatment that had not been answered by the lawyers or doctors. This was cultural: sometimes a doctor would tell a patient to eat things, like yogurt, that I knew Somalis had never heard of. Often when we left the medical building, clients would pepper me with questions: *What does this mean? What did that mean?* Sometimes they would complain that the doctor must be stupid, then ask me where they could get traditional Somali medicinal herbs.

I had become an expert on the Portland public bus system, but I knew I would need to drive a car someday, so I started taking a driver's education course. The class, at Yarmouth High School, was all teenagers. I couldn't believe the way they sat with their feet up on desks, talking over the teacher and throwing things at each other. You would surely be whipped in Somalia for such disrespect. I paid careful attention. The teacher was kind and helped me after class. When I was finally ready to start driving, the first thing I did was smash Sharon's car into her garage. It took me three times to pass the test for my license, but finally I became a safe and responsible driver. In November 2015, I had saved enough money to buy a used car, which allowed me to take even more jobs. Now my assignments doubled, and I was interpreting for court cases in both Lewiston and Portland.

One day I went to interpret at a dental center in Bath, Maine, about forty minutes up the coast from Portland. The patient was an elderly Somali woman, and her case-worker was the most beautiful girl I had ever met. She was tall, like me, with an open face and eyes that seemed curious to know all about the world. Half of her hair was uncovered, and she was wearing jeans with a light *dirac* on top. She seemed so outgoing and confident that at first I could not imagine she was a Somali immigrant. Her name was Fatuma, and she said she lived in Lewiston.

The old lady kept asking me about my tribe. We started discussing clans, animals, and life in the bush. Fatuma was just sitting there listening, but she had not said a word. I asked her to join our conversation, but she admitted her Somali wasn't very good and she couldn't follow us.

"A Somali who can't speak Somali?" I asked.

"I grew up in Vermont," she said in American English with no accent.

"So you are American?"

She smiled proudly. "My family came here when I was six."

Fatuma went to college nearby, earning a degree in social work. She was working for a public health nonprofit, as well as with a community service agency. She was more American than Somali, and for that reason her parents were pressuring her to be more a typical Somali girl, someone who stays in the house and knows about her tribe and her family's history. Fatuma had two cats and lived in her own apartment with some of her siblings; I had never seen a Somali with a pet. She even named her cats after her best friends from high school, such an American idea.

When I told her that I had been in the United States for only two years, she did not believe me. All she had been seeing in her work were newly arrived Somalis struggling to adjust. They would only talk about their tribes, but when Fatuma and I started talking, it was about movies we had seen, food we liked, and places we had hiked. It was just a typical American conversation, except with a Somali girl. That was a first for me, and the time flew by. Then the dental appointment ended and we said goodbye. A few nights later she texted me: "I like you. You are awesome!"

We got together for dinner a few times and began to develop a great friendship. I told her my life story and how I was the kid in Mogadishu known to all as Abdi American. She laughed so hard at the idea that I was already an American way back then. Every time we got together, Fatuma came with her hair showing and wearing pants. I told her she looked great. Her friends were American citizens; some were even white. They would have what they called girls' nights, and they would talk about makeup, clothes, and new music.

We took walks along the beautiful beaches of Maine; we drove to Vermont, where she showed me her old neighborhood in Burlington. I took her to Yarmouth and introduced her to my American family. Fatuma cooked traditional Somali samosas for Sharon and Gib; everyone liked her.

Then it came time for me to meet her parents. They had been in the United States for twenty years but preferred to stick to their Somali customs. Her dad had been an engineer in Somalia with a government job before the wars, but in Lewiston he didn't work; he spent his time in the mosque. Her mom was the breadwinner; she owned a store that imported all kinds of housewares and clothes for Somali immigrants. She traveled often to China, buying goods for her store.

I felt butterflies in my stomach the day I walked up to their house. Fatuma's dad was waiting outside the door. It was snowing, and frozen white flakes were sticking to his long beard like confetti. He shook hands with me and asked, "Did you pray today?"

I told him I did. He threw out several test questions about Islam, Somali culture, and places back home. I gathered he was not impressed by my tribe—his family was Darod—but I think he still respected me because he and his wife had lived in Mogadishu in the 1980s, so we all had Mogadishan accents. As soon as we walked inside, he took out his phone and asked me for my dad's number. He dialed my dad in Baidoa and talked for a few minutes. Then he hung up and called my mom in Mogadishu. Within an hour, all four of our parents had arranged our engagement.

Fatuma and I felt so betrayed. We both well understood that in Somali culture "engagement" is not some symbolic commitment; Somalis don't get engaged and marry two years later, like Americans. It's basically a wedding announcement. Like with my sister, Nima, an engagement means the wedding will happen as soon as the goats and camels can be rounded up for slaughter.

Fatuma and I certainly felt stirrings of that commitment, but neither of us was ready to get married anytime soon; we just wanted to greet her parents out of respect. Fortunately, Fatuma was not afraid to speak up to them. She told her dad to hang up the phone with my mom and that she wanted to talk to him and her mom in private. The three of them disappeared into the bedroom for several minutes. When they came out, her dad was frowning, and her mom seemed mad.

Fatuma's parents were about to move back to Somalia. Her dad had health problems that he felt were made worse by the cold weather, and they decided to move back to their home in Kismayo in southern Somalia, even though it was surrounded by al-Shabaab and not very safe. They had saved money and were hoping to start a fishing business. They tried to encourage Fatuma to come with them, but she refused. Her home was America. Now they were understandably worried about their daughter being left alone, even though she had nine siblings in Lewiston.

"How can we trust him with you?" her dad said to Fatuma, as if I weren't in the room. "We don't want this American thing where people sleep together without being married. We are respecting our culture and glorifying our religion."

Then he looked me in the eyes and asked, "What is your intention?"

"Fatuma and I have only known each other for a couple of weeks," I said. "When we know each other better, we will make our own decision. We don't need someone to make decisions for us."

This would have been unthinkable to say to Faisa's dad in Mogadishu all those years ago, but I was finding my American voice. Of course it helped that Fatuma was on my side. We were able to stand together and say no to an arranged marriage.

Even if we wouldn't marry quite yet, Fatuma was the person I wanted to be with. She was as American as the California girls I had seen in countless Hollywood movies. She had gone to an American public high school and college, lived in her own apartment with cats, wore blue jeans, had no accent and no concern about someone's clan. But she was also proudly Somali and had dedicated her life to helping other Somali refugees. Even if we weren't ready for marriage, we had talked about it and decided that we would definitely want our children to grow up speaking both English and Somali. We wanted it all, which seemed pretty American.

On my way home that evening, I thought of all my struggles in life. I truly loved my parents, but so many times I disobeyed them to follow my dreams. If I had listened to them, by now I would be an imam in Mogadishu, or beating kids in my own madrassa. Or, most likely, I would be a dead

Islamist soldier. In everything I did for myself, I never hurt anyone else. Was it disrespectful to do what I needed to do, say what I needed to say, in pursuit of my American dream? I didn't think so. And now, I felt I had so much to show for it. I had my work. I had Fatuma. My soccer mates and roommates, too. Far away as they were, I had my family. I had memories that would haunt me forever; but I also had the chance to make new ones in America.

EPILOGUE

In January 2017 an executive order was issued by the United States, barring citizens of seven countries, including Somalia, from coming to the United States. That included permanent residents with green cards, like me. I was advised by a lawyer not to leave the United States for any reason, because I might not get back in. It was a comfort to see Americans protesting against the ban, followed by court orders striking it down. But the damage was real and affected my own family just as I had feared. A few days after the executive order, my brother Hassan received a final denial letter from the U.S. embassy in Nairobi. It said, "As the request to review the case again has been rejected, the applicant has exhausted all avenues to seek a new decision on his refugee application and the original decision remains final."

My brother had now been a refugee in Kenya for fifteen years. Throughout that time he went back and forth for interviews to get resettled in the United States. Now his dream of coming to America is gone forever.

Hassan is now a husband and a dad of two boys and a girl. As a gift, I sent a thousand dollars for Hassan to get a twin bed and some cooking utensils, new clothes, and some jewelry for his wife. He went back to school after things calmed down in Little Mogadishu, and in March 2017 he got his undergraduate degree in community health. Sharon had paid his tuition. But today Hassan is back on the streets of Little Mogadishu hawking socks and shoes, struggling to support his family. In Kenya, refugees are still not allowed to work, even refugees with English and a college degree. My brother and his family have been granted asylum in Canada, but then Hassan was given a diagnosis of tuberculosis and has been made to wait until he is healthy.

Meanwhile in Mogadishu, my other nieces and nephews are growing up in the same civil war that has raged in one form or another for more than a quarter century. Somalia has changed little since I left. Al-Shabaab is active, and the African Union troops are still fighting them. Mogadishu has been reduced to rubble more than ten times. In October 2017, two truck bombs exploded in Zobe Square, the place where my brother used to hang out with his friends, killing more than five hundred people, including two guys I had played soccer with. In January 2019, al-Shabaab killed twenty-one people in a horrific hotel massacre in Nairobi. Just a few weeks later, a car bomb explosion at a shopping center in Mogadishu killed at least eleven people.

My sister Nima's children are growing up in the usual Somali way, living in a two-room hut. They go to the madrassa and get beaten so they will learn the Koran. My mom tells them the same stories that she told us about the nomadic life in the bush. Chasing the dik-diks, jumping over thornbushes, singing around the campfires, and praying for rain.

Omar, Nima's husband, no longer receives money from his cousin in America. Apparently, his demands grew too large after raising a family, and the cousin cut him off. He is jobless, wandering the streets of Mogadishu by day and returning home in the evening empty-handed. On May 8, 2017, his younger brother was killed in an al-Shabaab attack when they were walking together on the street.

Thanks to me, his kids don't have to beg for food. I do my best to keep food on their table and clothes on their backs, sending four hundred dollars every month. I know how hard it is to watch your own dad reduced to doing nothing in life. I trust at least they will not starve to death like my baby sister, Sadia, but a new drought in Somalia has driven up the price of scarce food, and I can send only so much money.

My dad is in Baidoa with three kids from his second wife. He calls to ask for money. Sometimes I can't help him; it is hard to support everyone. But the drought has touched Baidoa hard; it is very dry and hot there. People and animals are in pain and dying fast. How can I let my dad go hungry? So I send him what money I can to keep him alive. I tell him to bring his family to Mogadishu and stay close to my mom so they can eat together to survive. But the road to Mogadishu is under the control of al-Shabaab, and they kill people leaving Baidoa. He is stuck.

Macalin Basbaas is an old man now and can barely walk, but he takes small steps to our house to say hello to my mom. He often visits at the end of the month when he knows I send money to her. She gives him food and sometimes buys him clothes. And several times I have sent him money directly. This may seem hard to understand after all the cruelty he showed me, but it would stress my mom to see him in misery, so I have helped. I also realize that without him, I would never have memorized the Koran; those verses do comfort me every day. Macalin Basbaas probably does not remember cursing me when I wore jeans and listened to American music. Back then I was the stupid boy, the wasted student, not like my friend Mukhtar, his devoted assistant who died in jihad. Macalin Basbaas respects me now.

Siciid, my father's friend and our truck driver, died of natural causes. Falis, who introduced me to American culture in her video shack, also escaped Somalia. The last I heard, she was living in Nairobi, but I am no longer in touch with her.

In early 2017, I joined a group chat on WhatsApp with Faisa, who is living in the Dolo Ado refugee camp in Ethiopia. She sent me a private message: "Is this Abdi American?" In no time we were speaking on the phone. When I told her I was in the United States, she could not believe it. We talked about our memories of good times on the beach in Mogadishu, before al-Shabaab came and ruined it. Our first stolen kiss, under the mango trees and the chattering monkeys by the river in Afgooye. How life had changed for us. Faisa is married now to a man of her own tribe. She said she danced at her wedding. That made me happy, remembering our first meeting.

My mom is getting old. She can't see or hear well, and she has no way to get eyeglasses or hearing aids. But she can still run fast and jump high; brave Madinah is still strong. She dreams of a Somalia without violence so that she can go back to her nomad life. I dream of bringing her to America, just for a visit, so at least she can experience a different life. I would love her to see snow and fall foliage, and let her taste the many kinds of food. I would take her to some farms in America where they have cows she could touch and smell, even if they're big and fat, not like the skinny long-horned cows my mom and her family had. Then I would let her go back and spend her final days in her beloved bush, gathering the fragrant herbs of the desert, bathing under the Isha Baidoa waterfall, and calling out to camels and goats. People of her tribe still live that way in the twenty-first century.

In the years since I arrived in America, I have been on radio and television, in newspapers, and to conferences. I was a keynote speaker at the University of Maine and I talk often to high school students around the state. I have traveled to Seattle, Arizona, Minnesota, New York, Washington, DC, and many other places. Every time I tell my story, I am reminded how lucky I am to be here. Abdi Iftin, a child of war in Mogadishu, with no more formal education than Macalin Basbaas's madrassa, speaking at famous universities! Once I wanted to be like Arnold Schwarzenegger; now my idols are those students I meet. I have enrolled at the University of Southern Maine and plan eventually to study law.

In Somalia, at least the politics have become a bit brighter. Along with the U.S. elections in 2016 came a presidential election in my home country. The winner was a Somali American from Buffalo, New York. His government is still only provisional and is not in control of the whole country, but it is a start. Half of the people in the current Somali government are from the United States. Some of them can't even speak proper Somali; they grew up here. Somalis who came to America as refugees are returning as leaders.

No one from my Rahanweyn clan is yet able to run for Somali president. They are still considered lower class and unfit for the top job under the power-sharing system set up after independence in 1960. But the Rahanweyn are many, and politics can change. Someday I would like to be Somalia's first Rahanweyn president, but I want to run as a Somali American, not a Rahanweyn, promising peace and justice for all Somalis regardless of clan.

I want to land at Mogadishu Airport one day with a heart full of love and ambition for my people. Somalis overseas send back $1.4 billion every year to their families in the home country, according to a 2016 World Bank report. This is more than all foreign government aid. But I think we could do more. What if we could spend that money to start schools in Somalia, teaching more than just the Koran? What if we built roads, sanitation systems, hospitals, apartment buildings? Islamic extremism—which of course is not the same thing as Islam—is currently the greatest roadblock. Al-Shabaab prefers madrassas and child soldiers to clinics and colleges. And because they thrive on chaos, they love politicians around the world who shake their swords at Islam.

But radical Muslims do not represent Islam. Nor do they represent the hopes and dreams of the Somali people. You can pray to Allah five times a day and still hold hands at the movies, this I know. It is possible to savor camel milk and democracy, to chase dik-diks across the bush and stop at red lights, to proudly name your nomadic ancestors and dance to hip-hop at your own wedding. These are not contradictions or abominations but reflections of our universal humanity and, yes, our shrinking world. How else to explain an African boy's love of *Terminator* movies, or African drumming classes being taught in American high schools?

My passion for America was ignited by Arnold Schwarzenegger. Hiding from militia fighters in Falis's video shack in Mogadishu, watching the Terminator dispatch his enemies from the seat of a motorcycle, I had no idea that my hero had not even been born in America. Like me, he'd had a dream to call himself American since he was a child suffering abuse—in his case, beatings from a strict dad. Now I can see so many ways this poor boy from war-torn Austria was like the poor boy from violent Mogadishu. When Arnold was born, right after World War II, many people thought the countries of Europe were incapable of democracy; the same is said today about African nations. It took time, but finally many of those European nations, including Germany itself, became beacons of freedom and tolerance. I hope that holds, but more important, I hope that my own example reminds people of what is possible. No one gets to choose when or where to be born, but what happens after that is what you can imagine.

ACKNOWLEDGMENTS

I could not have written this book without the tireless support, prayers, and encouragement of my family: my mother, Madinah Ibrahim Moalim; my father, Nur Iftin; my brother, Hassan Nor Iftin; and my sister, Nima Nor Iftin, have all shared stories from my childhood and their own. While these stories were already a part of my life, my parents and siblings filled in countless details important to researching the book over many hours of phone conversations between Maine, Kenya, and Somalia. Often these stories were painful for them to recall, and I applaud their bravery in revisiting ugly memories. While shocking to Westerners, my family's continuing struggle to survive will be sadly familiar to millions of other Somalis—to those like me, who got out, and to those like my family, who remain behind.

I also want to graciously thank the team that came to my rescue when I was living in Mogadishu as a young man hunted by radical Islamists and other armed factions: Paul Salopek, Cori Princell, Dick Gordon, Ben Bellows, and Sharon McDonnell and her family made a dream team that set up a fund to support my family and my journey out of Somalia to Kenya and finally to the United States.

In Nairobi, special thanks to Pamela Gordon, who took risks to help me, and to my friends Yonis and Farah, for standing with me together and texting each other when we became prey for the police.

I am grateful to have a wonderful literary agent, Zoë Pagnamenta, who mentored this book and my writing so diligently, and the fantastic team at Knopf, including Andrew Miller, Zakiya Harris, and Bette Alexander. Thanks to Max Alexander for the passion and guidance he brought to this book. I am lucky to live in the same state as Max, and the work we did together on this book was remarkable. Thank you, Max, for being such a good and supportive friend.

Very special thanks to Sharon McDonnell and her husband, Gib Parrish, for their generosity in allowing me to become a member of their family and to write this book in their house in Yarmouth, Maine. I would not have been able to complete it without their moral and material support. Thanks to Becky Steele and her husband, Douglas McCown, for standing up for me and other Maine Somalis. Thanks to Kirk and Camille, who volunteered their time and ideas.

Finally, thanks to Nicole Bellows, Margaret Caudill, Leo Hornak, and the BBC, and to *This American Life* and

Ira Glass for following and documenting my story in Kenya and America. I also want to thank Elizabeth Harvey, Burhan, Gedi, Liban, Hannah Read, Maya Tepler, Gil Morino, Meg, Rick, Nene Riley, Shannon Sayer, and Natalya and Morgan McDonnell.

ABOUT THE AUTHOR

Abdi Nor Iftin is a radio celebrity, an award-winning author, a storyteller, a mentor for young writers in Maine, and a refugee advocate. He enjoys traveling and hiking in the woods.

callmeamerican.com

@Abdi_Iftin 🐦 📷

@CallMeAmerican 📘